TALES FROM THE SEA

BIRGER SJÖBERG

Prime Seven Media
518 Landmann St.
Tomah City, WI 54660

Printed in the United States of America

CONTENTS

PREFACE

The contours are dim but, every now and then, they become clear; the memory appears as suddenly as a gust of wind tearing apart a cloud of mist, peacefully resting on the sea. I am three weeks old, and my parents are bringing me to an island on the West Coast for the first time.

I lay on my back with the starry skies above, surrounded by plaited rattan, and watch as a high mast softly pendulates while gentle waves carry me across the sea.

The scent of diesel and the warm, August evening with its soft breeze augments into an imperishable feeling of safety, a memory which will always take me back to that enchanted period at the beginning of life.

This book is about a number of boats, ships and people that have crossed my path throughout the years. A never-ending wish for freedom and adventure fuelled my ambition to be part of different endeavours, such as renovating vessels of all kinds, while always maintaining the same goal — sailing towards the sunset.

The reckless voyages of my childhood in the skiff certainly solidified this extensive, (and expensive), yearning for conquering the seas.

As a young boy, I could still see sturdy wooden freighters carrying a variety of cargo through the archipelagos of Sweden, powered by semi-diesels or hot bulb engines, but now and again with their mighty sails hoisted, ploughing their way across the Skagerrak or the Baltic Sea.

And the dream was there to stay.

Finally, I was "cured" of my yearnings, but have kept in close contact with everything that floats. Throughout my years as a sailmaker, I have had the privilege of delivering sails to a vast number of beautiful boats and ships, thus taking part in somewhat more successful ventures than those of my own.

The dream of sailing ships and roaming the endless ocean will always occupy us, whether we have a boat or not. The reason why does not really matter, everything does not have to be explained.

Järvsö February 2024
Birger Sjöberg

THE GIFT

*We are tied to the ocean. And when we go back to the
sea, whether it is to sail or to watch – we are going back
from whence we came..."*

– John F. Kennedy

The boy gave half his Mars bar to the father. The July dusk lay warm over the grassy beach as they walked, side by side, down towards the jetty.

-You must have something in return for such a gift, said the father ceremoniously.

-It's good manners to share, said the boy. "Yes, but this gift from you means something special to me, the father replied."

The bay lay still, gently coloured by the setting sun of which a golden fragment was still visible over the top of the mountain to the northwest. They stopped at the gate and the father said:

-A few years from now, we are going to buy a big ketch and sail out onto the seas. I shall have to be the captain, of course, but you could be my first mate!

-That's great, said the boy, but couldn't we buy the ketch this summer?

-I have to earn some more money first, but all the same, there must be something you can share…

He bent down to the boy and whispered in a voice broken by emotion:

-The canoe! From now on you own half the canoe. We are going to share everything!

The canoe, which was rotten through, sank in the bay later that autumn and became a nuisance to the fishermen dragging for mackerel.
But for a short moment that night, the boy and his father were singularly close to one another and just then a dream took root in the boy – the dream of owning a ship.

THE SKIFF

In the last year of the reign of Charles XV, just in that first tender green of June, five pine trees sprung from their newly awakened seeds in the cleft at Bovik on the Hamburgö island in the parish of Kville on the Swedish west coast. They broke the soil just behind a big boulder and were left in peace by the hooves of cattle and the soles of men. The years went by and slowly but surely the firs grew tall and slender in the meagre soil. Hardened by January's frost and the draught of July, vigorous from their never-ending battle against the north wind, they acquired the qualities which eventually sealed their fate.

For all of sixty years they stood there, watching the passing seasons and people in their struggle for life. In a small gap to the northwest, they overlooked the sea and like silent watchmen they witnessed many events which should have been taken down: sturdy mackerel smacks going out with high

3

freeboards and coming back in loaded to the gunwales. Gayly decked narrow double enders on their way to some celebration, bustling inshore steamers and drowned seamen from the Battle of the Jutland.

Then, on the 20th of January 1932, fate fell upon them in the guise of Karl Olsson from Bovik. The regular beat of the log saw, and the adze travelled far in the clear air and after only a couple of hours they lay there neatly stacked and ringbarked. Twelve months later, the five logs were put through Karl's framesaw and meticulously padded with dunnage in a neat pile smelling of resin.

Another year of waiting followed.

At the time when Mrs. Olsson began the preparations of the dried fish for Christmas '34, Karl finally started the building of what would become a working skiff.

He had inherited some good molds for a fifteen-foot skiff from his father and it was not long before the garboard was ready and on Twelfth Night, several frames were already rough-hewed. By Easter, the outside planking was done and at the very beginning of May she was ready for launching. She lay there newly tarred, golden brown and shining, beneath the part of the roof extending from the workshop. Copper riveted in the modern fashion and with tholepins for two. Karl had built her on speculation, as they said, and he counted on being able to sell it at a good price to one of the summer visitors who at this period had just started to appear in the two little fishing villages of Hamburgsund and Fjällbacka.

A suitable day for launching was Mrs. Olsson's birthday, the 10th of May, and at noon that day they rolled the skiff out into the still spring sea. She lay nicely in the water and was so tight that she hardly let in a spoonful of seawater. Whether the skiff was ever sold to a summer visitor or not is not clear. What is true, however, is that she had to do her share of work and that she stayed in the archipelago between Tjurpannan and the Hamburgö island.

In the beginning of the fifties, she was bought by my father for one hundred and fifty Swedish crowns and became, at last, a skiff for summer visitors at Musö. Every summer she lay there peacefully rocking alongside the jetty, though rotten through and leaking more for every year that passed. Equipped with a notoriously unfaithful "Archimedes Marinoped" (a Swedish Seagull!) she was used mainly as a boat for net laying. But for me in my countless daydreams she became a ship that, whilst safely moored at her birth, took me away on endless adventures.

Finally, that fantastic summer came when I was considered mature enough to row her on my own and an intense period of restoration began. A friend and I hauled her up on the beach to give her a good overhaul. The worst cracks were tightened with boiled pitch and cotton yarn which in those days, in the early sixties, had become an increasingly common sight on the summer beaches. The pitch consisted of waste oil lumps from cargo ships in the Skagerrak. These lumps were a thorough nuisance to people as they stuck to shoes and clothes. But it was excellent for tightening old skiffs.

An extra plank was nailed onto the bottom to serve as keel and a steering-oar was lashed to the sculling hole. Sturdy bamboo poles, debris found on the beach at Musörumpan, served as masts and two cotton bed sheets were sacrificed to make sails. To us she was a full-rigged ship, and we baptized her "HMS Bounty" in a bottle of sparkling lemonade. During a few enchanted summers in the sixties, she took us out on perilous expeditions on the outskirts of the archipelago: the islands of Lönnholmen, Skårholmen, Otterö and Stora Borgen and as often as we dared, we sailed into the channel between Lökholmen and Dannholmen just to be able to wave to Ingrid Bergman and her children, Isabella and Robertino. As to her sailing qualities, she was at her best going before the wind and we often worked ourselves to death rowing her out to "Mormorsgrynnan", a sunken rock to the southwest, so that afterwards we could run home with the bamboo poles bent like longbows in the gale.

The very summer that the dreams of the Prague spring were crushed under Russian tanks, she finally gave up. Quietly and without ceremony, she simply refused to float. In a pathetic attempt to save our flagship we hauled her up on the beach where she spilled her rivets and opened up her planks to give up the ghost. The once so vigorous pines from Bovik had finally come to rest.

For a couple of years, she lay there on the beach, increasingly shapeless. The bottom_planking blended together with seaweed and sand, and it was only the still healthy rails that managed to maintain an appearance of form.

A late August evening in the early seventies, I took pity on her and let her depart from this life in a manner worthy of a king's ship. At first the flames hesitated, as if in awe of this sacrifice, but soon she was consumed violently and greedily by the fire. Large sparks rose in the evening sky, like released spirits and in a final sparkle two persevering frames collapsed and were devoured by the heap of glowing charcoals. And so, I mourned my first ship.

The last thing I did before it was time to return to my winter dwelling, was to scatter her ashes on the potato-patch.

M/S RUBENS

"To young men contemplating a voyage, I would say go."

Joshua Slocum

M/S Rubens
(Photo unknown)

M/S Rubens, Belgian America Line.

Weighing in at just about 10,000 tonnes, built in 1955 in Rotterdam for general cargo, but later rebuilt into a container ship.

Provence

C harley, Olaf, and I had just barely scraped together enough money for one-way tickets to the Great Land of the west. With our illusions somewhat tarnished, we were made to accept that our ambition of working our way to Tahiti, which was our goal, on a merchant ship was somewhat unrealistic. We just had to face the music: we would need to pay out of pocket for long stretches of our trip. This, alone, posed a tangible threat to our adventure.

Having already diminished a sizable and worrisome portion of our travel funds to rove around Europe, we also knew that our emergency solution of pleading to our families back home to subsidise us would have to remain just that, an emergency solution. A way to return home to Sweden quickly if one of us fell seriously ill.

Still, Tahiti was our destination, come hell or high water. We just had to make our money stretch!

During most of the last year and a half, the dream of Tahiti had been ever present. Daydreams, maps, and planning had a profoundly negative effect on my high school studies, and my mother's influence certainly did not help. Being a very wise woman, she encouraged me to go on with the planning, and every now and again she would say: "You can always catch up with your studies later…"

She went as far as ignoring the fact that I repeatedly skipped school and helped me find useful maps or plotted interesting routes with me. She was a remarkable woman. Quite frankly, my teachers let out a sigh of relief at the end of the semester, when I finally bid them adieu.

The key points of our plan involved that my two mates, Charley, and Olaf, were going to get tickets for themselves on the passenger ship *M/S Caledonian* voyaging from Marseilles to Papetee but bound for Australia. However, as I was lacking the necessary funds, I would be applying for work onboard, thereby fulfilling our dream of getting there together.

Ready for the great adventure

But things seldom work out as planned...

Anyway, this is how I found myself (a month ahead of my friends) alone in Marseilles, attempting to get a job aboard the *M/S Caledonian*. A challenge that I, in true youthful ignorance, considered to be a mere formality. Without a doubt, the captain of the Caledonian would hire a well grown and able Scandinavian young man to handle miscellaneous tasks onboard – and gratefully so! Unfortunately, this did not happen.

My second attempt resulted in a brusque eviction onto the gangway by two brutal sailors, who reassured me that I would get a good beating if I showed my face on the ship again.

Hurt, offended, and fully prepared to hitch-hike back home, I returned to the youth hostel, which was located in eastern Marseilles, not far from the old harbor. The commercial port of Marseilles is situated almost halfway to Cap Couronne, and it was a long and dusty road to walk. The bar L'Etoile, with its broken neon sign, lured me into its air-conditioned comfort. Here I could, for a while at least, drown my sorrows and soothe my battered self-esteem. After having downed some vodka and two sodas, I began enforcing a more philosophical approach to these disappointing events. The jukebox played Mungo Jerry's "In the Summertime", and my self-confidence slowly returned.

Life does not always deal you a good hand, I contemplated youthfully. Surely, I will find a way to get to where I want to go. Maybe as a stow away, if by no other means. And as it happened, destiny had its plans for me, serving up an offer I could not refuse.

Back in my room at the hostel, which I quite literally regarded as my own, my eyes caught sight of an unfamiliar knapsack. One of those new, square, tall, highly practical ones. Invented by some clever American, no doubt. Compared to my own, a worn out 20-year-old back-bender, this was a wonder of modern design. It was decorated with pennants from French vineyards and a huge Australian flag covering the top. On the other bed across the room, someone had placed a couple bottles of wine, a variety of cheeses, and a dildo-shaped sausage which was exuding an almost unbearable odour, reminiscent of decaying butchered animals and herbs.

The last thing I needed right now was a meddlesome roommate, occupying my precious time with gossip and an exchange of addresses. My frustration and disappointment induced a severe headache, so I threw myself on my bed and fell asleep instantly.

I was awoken by someone whistling out of tune. A Melanie-song, butchered by way of hoarse exhales. The smell of the sausage and never-washed hostel mattresses made me slightly nauseous, and I silently reminded myself of the idiocy of drinking hard liquor in thirty-five-degree summer heat. With a great deal of effort, I opened my eyes and there, in the backlight of the sole window, a young woman was brushing her hair.

"Sorry mate, I didn't wake you up, did I?" Her origin was in no way a mystery to me. With squinting eyes, I observed her for a few seconds; pale blonde hair and a pair of happy eyes, shifting in blue and green. She was breathtakingly beautiful.

"No, no, that's okay. I was just taking a nap," I replied and stood up, way too hastily, providing an opportunity for the six-inch nail, aka the result of my hangover, to hammer into my left temple.

"You don't look too good mate, stay right where you are, and I'll fix you up in no time!"

And, in no time, she set up an improvised meal on the bed, including three tablets of aspirin. As we ate, we began sharing our life stories. Her name was Susan, she was the daughter of a wealthy sheep farmer situated nearby Alice Springs in the Northern Territory. Soon, she was about to head home on the *M/S Caledonian* and put an end to a, for Australian youngsters, mandatory trip to Europe.

"Before settling down, one must experience the world, mate! See what's out there!" In between chews, she explained she would not have much time for travelling once she got back to the farm. Her parents were getting old and worn out after a whole life in the Outback. She continued:

"Now it's gonna be interesting to see if I can find a man with enough balls to share that kind of life with me!"

She let out a sudden, contagious laugh and poured us some more wine. Looking straight into my eyes, she continued:

"I can offer you a fine life out there… Lots of hard work, but also lots of fun, and rolling in the hay…"

After a minute's delay, I realised that I had just been on the receiving end of a proposal! Bewildered, words escaped me, and I ended up just looking at her while she cut some more slices of disgusting sausage. Clearly, she was a couple years older than me, but she had a certain type of charisma I had never experienced before. A child of nature, with a face full of smile lines and a zest for life beyond all limits. And, on top of it all, heir to a prosperous sheep farm. But, by God, we had only known each other for an hour...

She looked into my eyes, tilted her head a bit, and raised her eyebrows, insinuating that she was waiting for an answer. Her eyes maintained their gleeful air, but with a hint of seriousness.

"Do you mean that... you and I... but I'm going to Tahiti... and..."

She burst into laughter, and I wondered if I had just been the victim of a prank. She gathered herself, wiped the tears off her face, and sat down beside me.

"You must excuse me, but the expression on your face was priceless; completely panicked, as if I was going to eat you up... Although, mate, I am serious..."

She started rolling the stem of her wine glass between her hands and, for a few moments, she went silent.

A garbage truck thundered past outside, and a stray cat materialised itself on the windowsill, probably attracted by the smelly sausage. Gusts of hot city air found its way into the room, not doing much to improve the air quality. I was sweating profusely, and, on Susan's nose, pin-sized drops of sweat appeared.

"So... you don't think we've known each other for long enough... and feel it's all a bit hasty...?" After emptying her glass, she let out a deep sigh and continued:

"You see, I just can't visualise any of the blokes back home sharing my life with me... there's just a bit too much red-neck-thinking there..." She paused for a few moments, and I was still lost for words.

"And then I saw you lying there... a sleeping Swede..." She nodded towards my worn-out knapsack with the smallest of Swedish flags adorned on top.

"And heavily hungover, as it turned out... which just proves you can manage a drink or two and still be all right. And besides..." She hesitated briefly, but just long enough for me to be surprised by the display of a fraction of shyness.

"Besides, I like your looks..."

Before I could comment, she continued:

"And you've told me what you care for in life; the sea, animals, people... Also, you look like you could put in a hard day's work! And you have an easy laugh... that's enough for me, there's no need for me to go around scratching my head for months if the basics are where they need to be. We'll sort out the hurdles as they come!"

Although she radiated warmth and sincerity, maybe in a somewhat wild way, I could not help feeling like I was being regarded as a prime ram on the livestock auction in Wagga Wagga. But the notion of being wanted, needed, and my natural vanity, soon clouded all my senses. To hell with Charley, Olaf, and Tahiti! I was to become a sheep farmer in Australia!

"But..." I began protesting, lamely. "What would your parents say if you came home with an unknown Swede? Besides, we need more time to get to know one another... and, finally, I don't have the funds for a ticket to Australia..."

She interrupted me with an averting gesture, embraced me, and kissed me with great passion, annihilating my last lines of defence. Then, she resolutely pushed me away and stated:

"Listen to me, Burger. My parents will be overjoyed since they gave up on me and the prospect of future generations a long time ago." She took a deep breath and went on:

"As for your second concern, we've got two months to get to know each other. So, when we arrive in Tahiti, the matter of us two getting along should be quite settled. And, just for the record, I don't think we'll be leaving the cabin very often..."

Another kiss.

The combination of wine and her unique and confident way of coming onto me had profoundly stunned my sense of rational thinking. I was caught in an ocean of egocentricity, close to biblical proportions.

"As for your final concern, funds for the ticket, I've got enough money to pay for it, if necessary. However, there is a more challenging and exciting way to go about it..." Still wrapped in her arms, I tried to reach back to the surface of reason, just to get a grip of her intensions.

"I'll invite you onboard as a visitor the day before departure, and you'll hide in my cabin!" I resumed my attempt at getting my mind straight as she continued:

"It's as simple as that! Once we're out at sea... well... they can't just throw you off the boat, right? First port of call is Trinidad, and by then everything should be sorted out!"

I prepared myself for firing back. The mere thought of being caught by the two, far too familiar, brute sailors in the crew made me sober up. I could picture myself peeling potatoes across the Atlantic, just to end up pining away in a Venezuela prison.

"Listen, my love (apparently, I had adjusted quite quickly to my new civil status), I really don't mind... I mean... I'm totally bewildered by everything that you've just said, and I seriously think this is all meant to be..." I hesitated for a moment and tried to slow down my heartbeat. "...but I really must wait for my friends to arrive before I can give you an answer... I do owe them an explanation..."

"No worries, mate," she replied and launched one of her breath-taking smiles at me.

We spent the week waiting for my two friends together and, ignorant of our youthful folly, we slowly embraced the fact that we were falling deeply in love. The very same day that Charley and Olaf arrived, she moved onboard the *M/S Caledonian*.

I reunited with my friends at the train station. They had travelled nonstop, taking *The Northern Arrow* to Paris, and instantly hurling themselves onto a connecting train to Marseilles. In my newly adapted identity as an experienced globe-trotter, I found them to be a bit "fresh off the boat". Charley was wearing a pair of new, spotless khaki shorts and a tilted Aussi hat, whereas Olaf was wearing a US military jacket and smoking his Camels.

I, myself, visibly more experienced, was wearing soiled blue jeans, aviators, and, of course, smoking cigarettes which were preferred by the locals: Gauloises Papier Mais.*

Chilling out at Chateau D'If September 1970.
(Photo Olle Blomqvist)

But it was great to see them again. At Café Neptune in Vieux Port, we began catching up. Although, I carefully avoided revealing my amendment to our plan (prematurely). Everything was all right back at home, and everybody was curious about our trip. Olaf handed me an envelope with fifty dollars inside from my unfathomably understanding mother.

Once properly installed at the hostel, we spent the night thoroughly exploring the red district of Marseilles. We were repeatedly warned about spending any time in the Arabic quarters, whether it was during day- or night-time. So, of course, we found ourselves there on several occasions.

During the first night my friends and I spent together, we lost track of time and got locked out of the hostel. Consequently, we had to spend the remainder of the night on the beach but fell asleep quickly in the lukewarm sand.

Waking up, however, was brutal. An angry police officer armed with a machine gun poked us with it repeatedly while letting us know the consequences of remaining on the public beach (being thrown into his darkest cell). As the sun was mercilessly frying our aching heads, we hurried into an open café. Sipping on café au laits, we made plans for the day. Unanimously, we decided to spend part of our day on Château d'If, the old castle and prison located on an island just outside the port. The same place where the Count of Monte Christo spent many years locked away, all depicted in the novel by Alexander Dumas. A great place to contemplate our sins and cool down, away from the overheated, dusty town.

By 3:00 p.m. that same afternoon, we had an appointment with a clerk at the shipping office for *M/S Caledonian,* confirming cabins for Charley and Olaf (the lucky ones with paid passage all the way to Polynesia…).

A skinny, hawk-nosed official studied us aggressively and asked for their tickets. I admit feeling slightly envious, considering the ordeals I had to go through to join them onboard. Unaware of the imminent catastrophe, Charley burst out in spontaneous joy:

"Within a couple of days, boys, we'll be on our way to paradise!"

The somewhat creepy clerk finished examining the tickets and asked in French:

"And your return tickets, gentlemen?" I translated, puzzled.

"Which damn return tickets? Ask him what the hell he's talking about!" Charley's voice had a high pitch, something which commonly happened when he was faced with setbacks.

"Monsieur, what do you mean by that? These gentlemen have prepaid tickets and valid visas…" He cut me off before I could go on:

"Please tell the gentlemen that they are not welcome to the French colony of Tahiti unless they are in possession of return tickets or…" he paused dramatically. "…or can present me with the sum of ten thousand francs. Each, of course…"

"Of course," I repeated, paralysed, not knowing whether to laugh or cry.

I will refrain from describing the following days of confusion, anger, and despair. It would best be summarised as a never-ending streak of phoning and telegramming Sweden in futile attempt to save our voyage onboard the *Caledonian*. Charley was in a state of rage, fully prepared to declare war with France, Olaf was smoking way too many cigarettes, and I was oscillating between hope and despair.

Of course, it did not help when I told them about my own unconventional way of getting to Tahiti… or Australia. The thought of pursuing a life with Susan was firmly planted in my mind, and every time I met her, I could not help myself from perpetuating how she made me feel. I was truly in love. Faith had decided on my future as a sheep farmer outside Alice Springs, and nothing was going to change that. And nothing could really stop me. All I had to do was say farewell to my comrades, wish them good luck, and put my faith in Amor and the Australian immigration authorities.

But we were supposed to experience this adventure together – stick together, for better or for worse.

I did not see much of Susan towards the end. She told me that she wanted to spend her final days in Europe exploring Marseilles. The few moments we had together were characterised by sadness. She said she did not want to cajole me.

"Just make up your mind, mate. You know I'll be there for you, but it's got to be your choice."

The very fact that we did not spend a lot of time together then, made me lean in favour of my friends and our cohesion, and made my mind up for good, Besides, my mates kept reminding me of my family back home and what their feelings might be about my disappearing to live somewhere in the Australian Outback.

At 5:00 p.m. on Thursday September 24th in 1970, the *Caledonian* set sail, pushed by two small tugs until she entered the outer pier. In the backlight of the setting sun, there she stood on the aft deck, her hair flowing underneath her unseemly hat. She waved once. Only once.

And my heart ached.

We decided to hike through Provence and sleep on lavender fields under starry skies, drink wine, and eat baguettes with cheese.

We would sing songs beneath the olive trees and cool our feet in the clear springs of the Rhone valley. In short, purifie our young, sad, disappointed minds by means of the clean Provençale air, and finally decide on our next destination Antwerp, Belgium.

Hiking may sound fancy but is, in real life, exhausting and troublesome. Besides, there were not as many vineyards as we had thought. For two days, we had to endure severe thirst and dust. We spent our third night in an obscure hotel in the village Manosque. On arrival, the landlord gave us a suspicious glance and demanded payment in advance. In iron beds from the days of Napoleon II, we got an early night and slept in the following day.

After a short walk to the vicinity of Oraison, we stumbled upon a bus headed for Grenoble. Even Charley, who insisted on continuing the hike until we could discern the Alps in the distance, surrendered to the comfort of the bus. Indescribably relieved, we were headed north, going via the narrowest roads. Many drivers in Latin countries seems to harbor an improbable faith in patron saints i.e., the ones dangling from the rear-view mirror or the sun visors. With unwavering resilience, regardless of road conditions, they step on the gas while eagerly discussing the latest football results with a passenger behind them.

The crucifixes and flowerbeds placed along the winding roads, marking the sites of fatal accidents, somewhat deprived us of the pleasure of riding the bus.

After arriving in Grenoble, we hopped on a train headed towards Freiburg, located in southern Germany. We decided on resuming our ambitious hiking, this time through the Black Forest. Hiking trails from the Middle Ages would take us along beautiful roads bordering on medieval castles and virgin springs in primeval forests. On top of that, we would be able to stay the night in picturesque taverns, enjoying German beer, knackwursts, and feather beds.

We spent a whole day looking for the forest, and eventually gave up. All we found was sparse hillsides with sad looking pine trees, affected by acidification and deforestation.

Therefore, we decided to part ways and hitchhike to Antwerp separately.

Two days later, on the Tuesday of October 6th, we reunited at the Antwerp Central Station.

The ship

October 24th, Port of Antwerp.

The taxi came to a soft stop just a few meters from the quayside. An oily mist appeared over the sea, partly hiding the harbor sheds, and erasing all contours. Somewhere in the distance, the invisible fairway buoys of the river Schelde roared, a sound reminiscent of sad extinct mammals. The scent of this commercial harbor was acrid, with its mixture of rotting sea weeds, diesel oil and burnt coal.

Three travelling young men unloaded their backpacks at Pier 27 on this gloomy October morning of 1970. A rusty sign said, "Pier 27", and we assumed we were in the right place, but where was the ship?

A couple days earlier, we were collecting our tickets at the shipping office for The Belgian America Line on Boosmanlej 35. The official was a gentle and empathic man with radiating compassion. Bewilderingly enough, he did not seem to fully approve of young, beardless boys travelling the north Atlantic in November on a small ship like the *M/S Rubens*. They were one cabin space short and so, initially, we were told only two of us could be accommodated. Also, in accordance with maritime law, commercial ships were only allowed twelve passengers at a time. If there was a higher number of passengers onboard, the captain was required to employ a ship's surgeon (at great expense, of course). However, he claimed he might be able to persuade the third mate to share his cabin with the second mate, for the small sum of forty dollars (as well as our discretion). The two twenty-dollar bills vanished before they had a chance to land on the table, and I observed as he slipped them into in the left pocket of his vest.

A sudden gust of wind tore apart the sticky fog and revealed a dark row of ships some hundred meters down the quay, towards the river. Above us, the loud noise of cranes loading miscellaneous cargo, bound for distant shores.

"Just continue reading the names on the stern of the boats... Our ship must be here somewhere..." Olaf's voice was hollow and somewhat despondent. From time to time, I get carried away and start imagining that we board the wrong ship, only to be thrown off in Sierra Leone or sold as slaves to some remote emirate in the Gulf of Persia.

Charley, who eagerly trotted away a few meters in front of Olaf and me, suddenly caught eye of our transportation.

"Here she is! Cool! What a giant!"

And she really seemed like a giant in the cold November mist, but mostly due to her huge load of containers; three lengthwise and three perpendicularly, from the bow and stern to the mid-ship deckhouse. But *M/S Rubens* was a small ship, weighing in at barely ten thousand tons, flagged in Belgium and owned by the Belgian-America Line for scheduled traffic between Antwerp and Newport, USA, under the command of Captain A. De Groote. So, this was the ship that was going to carry us to the New World!

Loading containers.
(Photo: Olle Blomqvist)

Tall shoremen and sailors quickly shuffled back and forth across the deck, getting everything ready for departure. There was a combined noise of sledges and angle grinders with the dull, monotonous humming of the auxiliary engine deep in the ship's interior.

A young woman waved to us from the ship's bridge and shouted something undistinguishable. After a moment of hesitation, we went onboard. A fourth mate popped out from behind a deck cover and sceptically observed us while politely asking why we were travelling with the *M/S Rubens*.

"We've got tickets for America," Charley replied precociously.

The mate, still wearing an incredulous expression, invited us to enter the warm cabin, after thoroughly examining our documents.

The midship quarters for passengers were situated on the second deck. It consisted of two L-shaped aisles containing six cabins each, of which Charley and I came to share one whereas Olaf got his own, situated upstairs in the fourth mate's cabin.

The cabins were sparingly but tastefully equipped with wall fixed bunks, a small table with a drawer containing the ship company's stationary, two armchairs, and a narrow cupboard. A pale morning light shone in through two round portholes, and to the left of a wall mounted shelf, there was a bathroom. After unpacking, we all went on a tour around the ship.

Two beautifully decorated glass doors led us into a bar and comfortable lounge, with rattan armchairs and mahogany panelling, mostly covered by sun bleached photographs of the ship company's different vessels throughout the decades. In floor bolted pots, small palm trees thrived. A rattling seashell curtain separated the lounge from the dining room, flanked by a huge poster of Josephine Baker, wearing only bananas.

The 50's ambiance was overwhelming. At any moment, William Clausen could burst out and do La Cucaracha. The dining room was light and airy, with generously sized port holes providing a great view in all directions.

Sturdy mahogany tables, also bolted to the floor, were arranged in irregular rows, and neatly covered with white tablecloths. If it were not for the vague scent of diesel, we could have been in any respectable restaurant.

This far into the story, I think a summarisation of the food we had onboard is in place. People often speak of French cuisine, but seldom of Belgian. Probably because the French are better at marketing their art of food making. All the while Belgian chefs, without making a big fuss, create dishes that are as delicious, at least.

M/S Rubens was a Belgian ship, exclusively manned by a Belgian crew. This included the chef who, by the way, never showed himself outside of the galley, but made this voyage into an unforgettable culinary experience.

Breakfast (always served between 7:00 and 9:00 a.m.) was relatively plain in comparison to the other meals, but nevertheless always tempting, with its newly baked croissants and huge cups of café au lait. For luncheon (12:00 – 2:00 p.m.) and dinner (6:30 – 8:00 p.m.), five, often six, courses were served.

What follows is a typical lunch menu from *M/S Rubens* on its fifty-seventh journey across the Atlantic:

Hors d'oeuvre Varié
Créme Dubarry
Rôti de Porc avec Choux de Bruxelles et Pommes Mousseline
Plateau de Fromages
Cornet à la Crème.
Café/The

For the price of $200 per person, (plus a $40 bribe) we were to be transported all the way to America and fed like kings, over the span of eleven days. Fair, even back in 1970.

A waiter appeared without making a sound, nodded courteously, and let us know that lunch would not be served until 1:30 p.m. I glanced at my watch – 11:00 a.m. The last couple of containers were being loaded. The foremast, just moments ago wrapped in fog, was now fully visible. A pale October sun just barely succeeded in creating reflections that were bouncing off the crystal chandeliers.

Our tour continued on deck. Bearish chains securing the containers made it almost impossible to walk straight but, by mostly crawling, we managed to complete one lap around the main deck, thus satisfying our curiosity.

A distant pinging let us know lunch was served. All passengers had embarked and gathered in the dining room for our first meal onboard.

Captain A. De Groote was a very short man who had an impressively wide waist, which was probably a consequence of the Belgian cuisine and, not to forget, the fantastic Belgian Trappist beer, exclusively brewed by Belgian monks.

Dressed up in a parade uniform, he wished us all welcome onboard and proposed a toast for a safe journey across the sea.

As mentioned previously, we were a total of thirteen passengers (officially twelve). Besides us, the three young Swedish globetrotters, there were three elderly American ladies, three American gentlemen, a middle-aged German lady, and a young lesbian couple. The reason why I mention their sexual orientation is because their love, and expressions of love, came to affect us all throughout the entire Atlantic crossing. They willingly shared their passion for each other, always and everywhere onboard, which was kind of cute but somewhat unconventional in those days. Finally, "The Waving Lady", the one that greeted us from the bridge as we came onboard, was young… and beautiful.

The afternoon turned into night, and an impregnable October darkness fell over the North Sea coastline and Antwerp. A chilly breeze swept in from the northwest and a strange silence fell over the ship. A busy day's work and noise was replaced with a low frequency screech and a slight movement of the hull. Our boat was being hauled along the quay to the outer pillar.

Sat in the comfortable armchairs, drinking coffee and some Brandy, we silently waited for the next sign of departure; the rumbling sound of the main engines running. And there it was, creating a vague clanking from the bottles in the bar, spreading to every inch of the hull with its dull vibrations.

"Far out!" Charley commented enthusiastically and continued:

"We're leaving the Old-World boys… Our first ocean crossing of our journey towards Tahiti!" He paused, frantically chewing on a toothpick.

"The New World lays ahead. But first – this remarkable adventure!" He looked at us and uttered menacingly:

"Just think of it, we're taking just about the same route as the Titanic did…"

I shivered and glanced at Olaf.

"Not such a good idea to discuss old shipwrecks at the beginning of a voyage, Charley…"

Offended, and with a grumpy face, he finished the last of his brandy. I realised that Charley's meddlesome attitude towards everything and everybody, sooner or later would make us split up. But then again, crossing the Atlantic together could make us grow closer to one another. Olaf was the absolute opposite of Charley – silent and thoughtful in a wise sort of way that counterbalanced Charley's and my own somewhat pretentious manners.

The first mate came over to tell us that *M/S Rubens* was about to cast off in a few moments, and that we were all welcome to view her departure from the bridge deck.

At 9:30 p.m. on the Saturday of October 23rd, *Rubens* left the quay. A small tugboat appeared out of the cold, foggy drizzle. Like a stubborn terrier, it pushed us away from land and, with that, *Rubens* was headed for the English Channel.

The sound of the breakfast bell woke us up the next morning. The wind had increased and shifted to a north-west gale, the channel waters grey and inhospitable. At 5:00 p.m. we made landfall at Southampton for loading additional cargo. Twenty-four hours later, we hoisted anchor, left Europe behind, and set course for the New World.

Leaving the port of Antwerp
(Photo: Olle Blomqvist)

The cousin of Golda Meir

The Waving Lady had three big dogs: an Afghan called Tammer, a Border Collie called Milou, and a Bouvier de Flandre called Tarrow. Upon entering the Irish Sea, she let us all know that she had become seasick as a result of the heavy seas. A persistent nausea made it impossible for her to care for the dogs. Was there any chance that any of the three young Swedes, or perhaps the first mate, could help her walk the dogs on deck?

For whatever reason, I accepted this request right away, unaware that I had made an enemy of the first mate…

After being dragged around deck and getting rid of piles of faeces, I returned to her cabin.

"Come in…" I opened the cabin door and found her stretched out on the bed, wearing nothing but a negligee and a thin silk bath robe. Her forehead was covered with a wet towel.

"Everything's okay with the dogs, they're all relieved now. Is there anything else I can help you with?"

"Oh yes, Burger," she whispered and fired away a smile from underneath the towel. She patted the side of the bed with her hand and continued:

"Have a seat and keep me company for a while. I know I'll feel better if I have someone to talk to."

While the dogs settled, one in each corner of the cabin, I sat down on the edge of the bed. She smiled towards me again, making my heart beat a little faster.

"Come closer Swede. I'm not going to eat you up." Although I was not completely convinced, I would not dare to object and moved a bit closer to her.

"That's better," she said and put one of her hands on my thigh.

"Now, I'll tell you all about myself, and then you'll do the same." Her voice resembled the one of the pythons Kaa in Kipling's *The Jungle Book*, which made me transpire. I turned my head for a moment to wipe some beads away from my face.

"I'm sure we've met in an earlier life, Burger, which is why I think this is the beginning of a fantastic friendship!" She awaited my response.

"Eh… well, I mean…I don't think we've met before…"

My puzzled countenance triggered an infectious laughter from The Waving Lady, escaping her as she puffed up her pillows. She was more beautiful than ever.

"Well, Swede, in time we'll get back to that. For now, I'll tell you about myself! First of all, my name is Betty and I'm twenty-six… I'm married to a Belgian man who's waiting for me in New York. Basically, I'm a non-orthodox Jew," she paused for a second.

"In fact, one of my cousins is Golda Meir."

"Oh… really?" I was impressed.

"Yes, but I have many cousins," she smiled at me and continued:

"My family is very wealthy and, when my parents died, I started receiving a generous yearly allowance… And, once I've turned thirty, I'll get hold of the whole family fortune of three million dollars!"

She told me that she and her husband spent their time travelling the world, experiencing other cultures, trying various smokable stimulants, and investigating all kinds of New Age movements. Their dream was to buy a sailing ship to travel the vast oceans. Their philosophy was to gather more people, cool ones, to make this dream come true...

As it turned out, their dream would overlap with my own, and come to affect a lot of people in ways I could not foresee or even dream of.

The hours went by, and we continued sharing our life experiences. She started pulling a couple bottles of wine and a well cured Camembert out of a huge trunk. Imperceptibly, our conversation slowly changed character, and as the amount of wine decreased in the bottles, my confidence increased. I could not be mistaken as far as what her intensions were. I was defenceless. She had made up her mind about seducing this young, inexperienced Swede. She had dark hair the length of her shoulders, brown and eager eyes, an upturned nose, and a sensual type of charisma, completely unbeknownst to me in my short seventeen years of life. When the evening turned into night, our conversation was over, and I got an overwhelming lesson in the art of lovemaking, which took forms I had never even heard of before. Somewhere in the middle of our embrace, we realised that the three dogs stood in a row by the bedside, closely watching us with their heads tilted. This somewhat disrupted my concentration.

In order to shift their attention, we gave them some dog chews.

During the remainder of the trip, until November 2nd, we were lost in an amorous haze. My travelling companions, at first impressed by my love life, soon got tired of my worn-out, rose-cheeked presence. *M/S Rubens* journeyed ahead at good speed across a relatively calm sea within a grey haze, which was every now and again replaced by a pale sun. When not occupied by each other, Betty and I socialised with the rest of the passengers, killing time with games of chess, walks on deck, and consumption of their fabulous cuisine. On the last day of October, just in time for lunch, Betty freed herself from my arms, looked straight into my eyes, and declared:

"Now, Burger, it's time for a party!" Wearing only her negligee and a thin robe, she went to the kitchen and returned with a bowl of mussels and four beers.

"I have just informed everyone onboard to dress up in costumes tonight!"

"Huh?"

"Well, it's Halloween, after all!"

"Hallo-what?"

"Halloween! It's an important holiday for us Americans. We wear scary costumes and walk around town, frightening anyone that isn't wearing one!"

"Again – huh?"

"Yes, and we knock on doors and shout 'Trick or Treat!', which, if the houseowner cares about their house, makes them give you candy or a glass of bourbon, depending on their age."

"That's something we definitely don't have in Sweden. Such a tradition would never be established at home! We celebrate All Saints' Day by lighting candles and placing them on the graves of our departed. Perhaps we'll have a nice dinner, as well."

She had an astonished look on her face and wondered if we, at least, decorated our houses with skulls or paper ghosts.

"No, heavens, no! Back home we have serious traditions rooted in our cultural heritage!" For some reason I felt a need to emphasise the values of the Old World. She was not impressed by my pompous attitude and burst into a contagious laugh.

"Okay, Burg. But we'll be in the States soon. Maybe you can go a bit wild and crazy and dress up tonight…?"

I felt a bit offended, but as my preconceptions had not yet had hardened into principles, I yielded. I simply could not bear the thought of not joining her at the party and decided on dressing up as a pirate. A choice I have continued to hold on to whenever I'm forced to participate in any sort of masquerade.

The evening was unforgettable. A somewhat grumpy Charley turned up as Caesar, Olaf was dressed up as Superman, which really cracked me up, whereas Betty being dressed as a fairy made my head spin. I could spot yet another pirate, two Napoleons, and a few miscellaneous Belgian fairytale characters. The first mate, who would not talk to me ever since the night he was rejected by Betty, caught her attention, and desperately tried to impress her with his version of the cartoon character Barbapappa. After several failed advances, he grumpily disappeared to the bridge to relieve captain De Groote of his duties, who soon after appeared as Neptune.

Our wild partying went on all night, and the first of November greeted us with a hazy sun and shifting winds.

The storm

Monday, November 2nd; two days left of our journey across the Atlantic. Betty had an urge to meditate and write letters all day long, and I felt the need to talk to my fellow travellers and map out the future. She had, from day one, eagerly tried to convince us to join her and her husband in Colorado.

"You just have to get your asses over there! You can hunt and dig for gold! And we can take a trip to California to meet all our hippie friends. Jacob knows a former CIA agent in Pasadena that sells the world's best marijuana!" She fixed her dark brown eyes on me and finally, irresistibly, said:

"Afterwards, if you still want to, you can continue on to Tahiti… and do whatever you're planning on doing there…"

Considering these excellent prospects, I was determined to persuade my friends to tag along.

After dinner, the three of us went out on deck and had a lively discussion about our options. Charley would not hear of Colorado. We were going to Tahiti, and that was the end of it! Period! Olaf hesitated, but finally reached the conclusion that it sure would be nice to experience the US while we were there.

The second mate suddenly appeared out of the comms room, rushing by us with a piece of paper.

"He looked terrified…" Olaf lit yet another Camel.

As it was the day after the Halloween party, we were all hungover and had little to no awareness of the surrounding world, struggling to notice the strange change of weather. There was a creepy calmness, only interrupted by small gusts of wind coming from different directions. The sun disappeared into pitch dark clouds, which made the skies completely merge with the still, oily seas. Finally hit with the sensation of imminent danger, we headed to the upper bridge deck, housing a big wooden steering wheel and a binnacle with a spare compass.

"What's going on?" Charley's voice disclosed the fear we all felt.

"This certainly does not look good – I'll run down and check the barometer." Olaf disappeared down the ladder.

"I wouldn't be surprised if we were heading right into a storm." My voice was filled with a mixture of fear and anticipation.

The sea was calm now, black, and oily with a slow swell. And the air was completely still, as if we were inside a room with the windows shut. I looked at the compass and concluded that our course was steady, at a western 280 degrees, just as it had been for the last couple of days. The rumbling from the main engine suddenly sounded desolate, ominous. Olaf returned:

"The barometer points straight down right now... For whatever reason..." With a strained voice, he continued:

"And weird things are going on down there. The waiter is spraying water on the tablecloths and securing loose objects..." He paused and eyed his cigarette butt.

"And... the captain has posted a note on the bulletin board that reads: *"Your captain is regrettably compelled to inform all passengers that we are heading into a heavily low-pressured area, which can cause certain inconveniences. Let me ensure you that the crew will continue to do everything in their power to make the remaining passage as safe and convenient as possible."*

The Storm
(Photo unknown)

"That was smoothly put," Charley mumbled. We remained silent on the upper bridge, caught in the stuffy, steadily increasing darkness. A spooky, greenish glow appeared from the main bridge, and it seemed like we were moving into a tunnel. We twitched as a flash of lightening lit up the sky not far from us, and realised it was time to head inside. By the lifeboats, we passed the captain, apparently on his way to the bridge. He was a man with natural authority, achieved by many years spent at sea. He told us that our hair might become a bit frizzy in the coming hours. But it was nothing to worry about.

His aura of safety and competence had a soothing effect on us, so we bid each other good night and went to our cabins.

What made me stop and take a step back to glance through a porthole, I do not know. The captain remained on the lifeboat deck, his never-lit pipe between his lips, fully occupied with checking and securing the port-side lifeboats winches...

Olaf and Charley had disappeared into their cabins, but I remained in the corridor for quite a while, feeling slightly nauseous. Betty was already in bed when I entered. She drowsily shuffled herself towards the bulkhead, and I laid down on top of the covers without taking my clothes off. I decided not to sleep. In melodramatic seriousness, I decided to be ready for whatever was coming. I had experienced heavy storms on my childhood summer island, defying terrifying seas in my old fishing boat, wild passages across the bays in the breezy archipelago of the Swedish west coast. I knew the innermost essence of the sea. And I was ready and fell asleep.

Betty had a rough go at waking me up:

"Wake up!" She was shaking my shoulders in panic, her face greenish. A mere moment later, she rushed into the bathroom. A loud crashing sound followed by a strange, unnatural movement of the ship made me wide awake. I glanced at the clock above the cabin table, it was almost dawn. Everything had become chaotic. The change in the ship's movements felt unreal and terrifying, the whole cabin seemed to be caught in surrealistic turbulence. I fumbled for support and felt an immediate hit of nausea intermingled with chock waves of adrenalin. I could hear violent vomiting coming from the bathroom, but decided I could not help her. I just had to find out what was going on.

The corridor was an inferno of broken glass, books, and sea water. A beautiful bookcase with glass doors had dislodged itself from its bolts in the bulkhead and shattered. Charley stood in the doorway, painstakingly holding on to the doorpost.

"Shit, Burger, it's all going to hell!" His breathing was shallow, and his eyes were filled with panic.

"This is all happening because we're on the same route as the Titanic!"

In the very same instant, *Rubens* took a nosedive straight into a monstruous wave. I had just the time to think "How long is this fall going to take?" The crash that followed was terrible, the ship rattled furiously, and a series of sharp bangs indicated that something was very wrong, and very broken. In a slow pendulous motion, she straightened back up, only to start climbing the next mountain of water. Everybody was awake now, they slammed open their doors and came out wearing only their bath robes, holding on to anything they could, paralysed by fear.

Eighty nautical miles south of Cape Sable, Nova Scotia, *M/S Rubens* was facing a severe storm, bordering on full hurricane, with waves higher than her main bridge. A fragile bunch of people exposed to the elements, all of us at the mercy of captain De Groote's seamanship, gathered in the dining saloon.

There was no sign of Olaf, so I rushed to his cabin only to find him in bed in the middle of dealing with gruesome seasickness.

"Try to drink something," I suggested, in an attempt to encourage him. He mumbled that he was too sick to be afraid of anything.

"All right, I'll come back and check in on you later."

I ran back to the saloon, fending myself against the walls. *Rubens* rolled and heaved violently, creating sounds that were almost unbearable, but she seemed to get out of every impact in one piece. Waves breaking all over the midship construction demolished several doors and created rivers of seawater all the way into the dining room, which was profoundly demoralising for all of us. Every time the ship took a dive from the top of the giant waves, the propellers broke free of the sea below, which made the hull shake violently.

Betty showed up, green faced, declining all offers of help, told me to go to hell, and cuddled up in the saloon sofa. The chef, who we now got acquainted with for the first time, appeared out of the galley, parrying all movements with his sea legs. With an inscrutable expression on his face, he observed us all for a brief moment and said:

"There will be no warm lunch today," he parried another heavy roll of the ship and continued:

"Things will be getting a lot worse before they get better, but..." He smiled:

"I can recommend our excellent cold cut buffet!" His soothing remark about the excellence of the buffet somewhat appeared in sharp opposition to the fact that things were going to get even worse.

"What do you mean WORSE!?" the German lady shouted while clinging on to her handbag and life jacket.

"It cannot possible become any worse than this!"

The chef shrugged and returned to his kitchen. Everybody was upset now, and a loud discussion erupted and went on for quite a while; until Charley suggested that we should fetch the captain or at least send someone to the bridge for information about what kind of imminent danger we were in. One of the American ladies, probably the calmest of us all, said:

"I think captain De Groote has his hands full right now, so let's make the best of our predicament. I, myself, will be praying to the Lord that I'll get to see Pittsburgh again..." She stopped herself abruptly as we all started to feel it; *Rubens* had started climbing, as if it were in the grasp of a giant's hand, slowly, in a never-ending motion. Captain De Groote steered straight into the wind and waves, against this south-westerly storm that had originated at Cape Hatteras on the coast of North Carolina. It was building its force and fury now and would not reach its culmination for many hours.

The upward motion was overtaken by a heavy roll to port, after which the hull fell forward, picking up an unreal, frightening speed, only to have her ten thousand tons crash into a wall of water at the bottom of the wave. It is meaningless to try to attempt describing the sound and feeling of such an impact between steel and water. It must be experienced. Charley was right, this was the end. Finito, bye-bye.

A strange insight came over me, the realisation that I, at only seventeen years old, together with my comrades in despair, were to be claimed by my maker, never to return home to my family, only to be remembered on a brass plate at the cemetery back home.

Dawn broke slowly, the wind showing no sign of calming down. On the contrary. With frightening force, gusts of wind tore the sea's surface into a blinding curtain with repeatedly recurring waves, one higher and more powerful than the other. An ongoing, raging fury – nature's way of showing us its might. While the waiter desperately struggled to serve us some coffee, me and Charley decided on trying to get to Olaf's cabin. In the corridor, we bumped into the first mate. His looks convinced us even more of the end being near. His otherwise well-groomed hair was messy, his eyes were enlarged and brimming with anxiety, several buttons on his uniform had been torn off, and his chest was stained with spilled coffee. He was on his was to calm the passengers.

I had to shout at the top of my lungs to ask him if everything was under control.

He looked at me as if I had lost my mind, shook his head, and rushed into the saloon. In cold sweat and while seasick, we made it to Olaf's cabin. He was awake but in a miserable state, with his hair stuck to his forehead and his lips cracked.

"Can you guys get me a cigarette...?" His voice was more like a croak than that of a living human.

"How about something to drink instead?" Charley replied. "I can fix you up some broth from the galley."

Olaf's eyes turned inside out, and he began throwing up green slime in heavy convolutions.

"Goddamn it, Charley, choose your words! Get him a cigarette. It doesn't matter, we may all be dead soon anyway!" My intelligent comment made Olaf moan and cover his face with his hands.

We remained in Olaf's cabin, as we reckoned, we might as well be together until the end. From the deck, we could hear thumps of bursting lashings and the heavy chains holding the containers snap, resulting in the loss of the top layer of the deck cargo.

After a while, the fear was mixed with admiration of this little ship. Her welding joints enduring the vast poundings from the waves. And the main engine keeping up, struggling to keep *Rubens'* head facing the storm. Thanks to my acquaintance with several ship captains, I later found out that a modern cargo ship is designed to withstand almost anything, with proper seamanship of course.

I decided to do something insane.

"I'll step outside for a while..." Charley and Olaf stared at me in disbelief but, before they could object, I went out into the corridor. The transept, in front of the saloon and galley, was a gangway with doors leading out to where the lifeboats were. I stepped out on deck on the leeward side, persistently holding on to the railing. I wanted to see it with my own eyes, witness the wind and the roaring seas. I curled up behind a trunk of life jackets and observed the theatrics. Beyond the blinding foam, I could see the monstrous seas in all their might. Many have tried, in words, to depict this natural phenomenon. Maybe it is not meant to be described in words. Synonyms like "big as a house" or "mountains of water", are insufficient.

Millions of tons of ocean, moving at high-speed toward its own destruction against the rugged cliffs of Nova Scotia and New Foundland.

We are all very small out there. The water that we originated from covers three quarters of our planet's surface and could be the most simultaneously rewarding and devastating phenomenon in our existence. If the ocean was an independently thinking organism and got tired of all our oil spills, milk cartons, poisonous waste, and over-exploitation one day, we would, all of us, have to move to higher grounds. The hours I spent there on deck, behind a trunk of Belgian life belts, will forever be the mightiest experience of my life. Neither anything sooner nor later can compare with those twenty-four hours on the Atlantic, all those years ago.

From the documentation available at the Swedish Meteorological Institution concerning the weather conditions on the American east coast during November in 1970:

> *"...it wasn't considered a tropical storm that had deviated to the north, but rather a midlatitude cyclone. November 2nd, 1970, a rather weak low-pressure system arose east of Cape Hatteras. It deepened rapidly, moving towards north-east.*
>
> *On November 3rd, the low-pressure centre was located just south of Nova Scotia, several ships reporting a force of 11 winds with several hours of hurricane force at 12 and above. No heights of waves were ever reported, but judging by the character of the low-pressure we estimate the average wave height to have been approximately 10-15 meters..."*

Towards the evening, we all noticed a slight change. Not that the wind diminished, or that the waves reduced in height, but still... The raging fury seemed to have decreased. Like an exhausted boxer on their fifteenth round, the waves seemed to have given up their mission of destruction, letting the *Rubens* get away this time. Risking their lives, the crew tirelessly had fought the elements to secure the containers stowed on deck. Despite their efforts, half of the top layer of containers had gone overboard. The chef miraculously managed to conjure forth some hot broth, bread, cheese, and some of his beloved cold cut meats. Olaf was feeling much better and sipped on some broth. By midnight, the storm had decreased to a force eight gale and, although the ship still rolled heavily, we could resume our final course towards New Jersey. Less than seven hours to go.

I went to Betty's cabin and instantly fell asleep on her couch, although she soon woke me up, before any customs officers came onboard. She explained that she could be accused of raping me, since she was twenty-six, whereas I was only seventeen...

So, I went to mine and Charley's cabin and fell soundly asleep right away. For the first time in a week, in my own bed.

The author at the binnacle
(Photo Olle Blomqvist)

America!

The North American coast materialised in the morning mist. A soft breeze carried scents of landfall as we silently stood along the railing and experienced what countless travellers had witnessed since the days of Leif Ericson.

America. The word itself makes the heart beat faster, while diffuse expectations swirl around in your head. What did we expect, really? An infinite adventure, impossible to grasp. An uncharted world for the three of us, a new frontier. As it were, at this very moment, we might as well have been standing on the deck of the Mayflower, our senses wide open for any impressions to come.

Tahiti was our destination. The world of our dreams and fairytales. But standing there by the railing, seeing the New Jersey harbor appear in the haze, reality caught up with us and we realised the obvious: we had reached America, The United States of America! Who needs Tahiti!?

A small tugboat slowly manoeuvred The *Rubens* alongside the quay. A last shivering of the hull and she came to a rest, moored with coarse ropes to the New World. The quay was cluttered with piles of containers and resembled a cubist mountain landscape, divided by truck roads. A grey Jeep marked "Customs" made a stop at the gangway and three officials in uniform came onboard. Reality caught up with us and we asked ourselves the nerve-wracking question – were we going to thread the needle?

A few days earlier, the first mate maliciously informed us that we were required to present customs with a sum of one hundred dollars in order to be allowed entry into the country. One hundred dollars! I barely possessed thirty-five. Olaf had forty and Charley, for all we knew, had one hundred and fifty dollars in personal traveller's checks. Fortunately, we had come up with a strategy. We were going to be called into the customs offices one by one for our passport and visa control, where Olaf and I would show them the one hundred dollars that we had previously borrowed from Betty. Our plan felt unsafe, but there was no other alternative. What if all three of us were called in at the same time?

The moment of truth had come. At 10:30 a.m. on the morning of the 4th of November, we would find out if our trip would continue or come to an immediate halt, which would entail we would have to return to Sweden, courtesy of the consulate.

The officials had benched themselves behind the bar. Several different stamps of different sizes were arranged in front of them in a row. A chair facing the representatives of US Immigration awaited each of us and the other ten passengers. A court room feeling came over me. We waited in the passage between the bar and the dining room, last in line, nervously chatting. The rest of the passengers were American citizens and had nothing to worry about. For them, this was a mere formality. Our destiny hung in the balance; how strict would they be? Would they discover that we were underage? And what about the visas, were they valid...?

We did, however, have a card up our sleeves. Charley had relatives in the small town Rockford in Illinois, and my own brother lived in Los Angeles. Someone had told us that Americans have a soft spot for family ties....

The German lady came out of the bar waving her passport and shouted, with an ominous voice:

"They're waiting for you boys..." During the entire crossing she had, for unknown reasons, been quite hostile and continuously maintained a social distance.

Charley happened to be first in line and Olaf gave him a light push. He took a deep breath, gave us one last glance, and went in. The minutes went by slowly, very slowly.

"What's happening in there? This is going straight to hell!" He put out his cigarette and lit another one.

"What happens if they won't let us in? I just couldn't endure being sent home, not now that we've come this far!"

My throat was dry, and Olaf's anxiety made mine double in size. Usually, he was the calmest of us and never showed any signs of nervousness. Presently, he was in a state of dissolution.

"It'll be all right, Olaf. I know it! They just have to make sure everything's legit!"

My voice sounded unnatural and not even a little bit credible. Olaf took a step forward to sneak a peek and see what was going on behind the glass doors. A lavish design out of roses in the shape of a compass with intricate loops of seaweed patterns covered most of their surface.

At that exact moment, the door leaf hit him on the forehead as Charley opened the doors and returned to us. I stared at Charley for a few moments since his facial expressions were easy to read. And there it was, pompous contentment and an air of superiority. Olaf was cursing away with his bump growing larger on his forehead and went to the galley for some ice.

"No problem boys, it's cool! Just told them we're going to my relatives in Illinois! They've checked, so everything's all right!"

I quickly checked my passport and the borrowed hundred dollars in my pocket and went into the bar.

"Please sit down, sir." The official in the middle made an inviting gesture towards the chair. A few seconds passed before I realised, he had called me "sir".

My heart was beating so fast, and my throat was completely dried out, something I tried to resolve by repeatedly swallowing. They were all busy browsing through some binders, paying no attention to me. One of them selected a document, read through the text, and rammed it with a stamp as the next officer signed another one. The seconds passed and I started to wonder if this was some kind of psychological test. A test of how much doubt and uncertainty I could endure before I broke down. Cowards just were not going to be admitted into the greatest of nations.

"May I see your passport, please?" The man in the middle looked me straight in the eyes, his piercing gaze fixated on my eyes and soul, as if to judge the inner me. But not in a rude way.

"Yes, of course…"

I then realised what a bad accent I had, it really had to be improved. I did not want to sound like a Swede trying to speak American English. Up next, a range of questions followed: How long would I stay in the country? Whom was I going to visit? With a sense of triumph, I gave him the names of Charley's relatives, which did not seem to impress the least. Not even the fact that I had a brother in L.A. had an impact on the tribunal. How much money did I have? I handed over the sweaty roll of dollar bills and traveller's checks, totally convinced that they would call my bluff. With a bang that had the sound of a rifle shot, the final stamp landed in my passport.

"Have a nice stay in the United States, sir!" Three authoritarian faces smiled politely at me. My answer ended being a Swedish "Thank you". Their bewildered faces reverted into smiles as I repeated the phrase in English. In the hallway, Olaf was frantically biting his nails, as he was out of cigarettes.

"Your turn," I said after clearing my throat, and handed over the dollar bills.

Half an hour later, we stood on solid ground in New Jersey, North America.

For quite a while, we remained on the quay, imbibing the feeling of relief and success. All passengers were scattered in different directions. One cab after another came to pick them up and headed towards unknown final destinations. Betty and her three dogs joined us as the last passenger disembarked the ship. Her husband's arrival was imminent, and she had promised to find us some cheap accommodations. So, I was forced to meet her husband. Regardless of all her assurances that their marriage was "free", I could not help trembling, wondering what life had in store for me this time. How magnanimous could he be?

A gentle drizzle swept in from the sea, and the sound of engines, cranes, and trucks manifested. Just another day of commerce in the harbor. Out of the mist, an old VW bus approached. With a final backfire, it came to a full stop. A huge man stepped out, 6′5″, dark hair, and clean shaven with his shirt partly buttoned, exposing a hairy chest.

"Hi, love!" she shouted and disappeared into his arms. I had difficulty swallowing. Charley and Olaf alternated between eyeing their own shoes and the grey skies above.

"Well, Jacob, here are my new friends!" Betty excitedly explained while trying to manage the dogs who were entangling her legs.

"This is Charley, and here's Olaf, and that's Burger, my new lover!" I could not feel the ground underneath my feet, and small drops of rain seemed to evaporate as they landed on my head.

"Great to meet you all!" He exclaimed with his dark voice and distinct French-English pronunciation, before embracing all of us in one big hug. Then he turned towards me, his clothes exuding an exotic, sweet scent:

"And hey, man, thanks for taking care of my wife! I really dig that!" This was followed by a boisterous laugh. With all three knapsacks in one hand, he pushed us into the bus.

Our voyage across the Atlantic had come to an end. A new journey had just gotten started, over mountains, through forests, and deserts.

But that is another story.

SPIRIT OF CHICAGO

Together we knew the desolation of the great sea.
We saw the moon leap silver from the high wave peaks.
And watched the red sun die in a
welter of mist on the horizon.
All these things: the dizziness of struggle, straining
muscles, weariness, exaltation, the soothing
fragrance of the sea, the chatter of tiny wavelets,
and the furious roar of monstrous waves,
entered into the pattern of our
friendship and made it fine.
These things we knew together,
And these things we will remember ...

*Don Blanding **

(Photo unknown)

Two masted "Galeas" (Baltic Trader), launched in 1905, originally named *"Viking"*. Overall length: 20 meters. Beam: 5 meters. Originally built for carrying sandstone across the Baltic Sea. In the '60s, the rig was changed into that of ketch: gaff mizzen, gaff main, jib, inner- and outer jib.

Just before WWII, she was fitted with the main engine she had until the end; a one-cylinder, semi-diesel Hundested, 25 hp.

I had just turned sixteen when my family decided to move to the picturesque fishing village of Viken by the southwestern coast of Sweden. It is still a very nice place, but hardly a fishing village anymore. Due to the monstrous fishing factories that roam the seas nowadays, the small-scale fishing boats are all gone, along with their captains. At this time, my sailing ship experiences were not much to show for, but I was used to the sea and had been handling small sailing- and motor vessels all my life. Whenever I caught sight of a sailing ship, I was inexorably drawn to it. For whatever inscrutable reason, I had gotten stuck with the idea that the sea, in whatever shape or form, was going to dominate my life.

And during the first day in my new home, my eyes immediately caught sight of a beautiful sailing ship down in the harbor. Every chance I got, I sneaked past it, studying every detail of her hull, rigging, and deck layout. The villagers informed me of its owner; a shady character named Pekka. I soon realised that everything that was about him were rumours, difficult to verify.

He was seldom seen or even spotted by anyone, and I was advised not to approach him, to let him be. One of the most common tales about Pekka was that he had smuggled weapons for the IRA and done some serious time in jail for it. It is also very likely that he had been smuggling alcohol across the Baltic Sea using his old ship.

Drying the sails
(Photo unknown)

None of this had any deterring effect on me. On the contrary. I made myself a sacred promise to get to know this man and maybe, just maybe, sail with him – even if it were only for a short crossing of the Öresund Strait. Every day, before and after school, I spent hours strolling back and forth by the ship, enjoying her adventurous spirit (and looking for an opportunity to introduce myself).

Spring turned into summer, and I had yet to meet this mysterious man, finally leading me to believe he had taken off – left his old ship and vanished. Maybe on the lam from the IRA or the police. Then, on a peaceful and calm morning in June, I decided to skip school and spend the entire day in the harbor. As my mother had long since given up on my academical career, she let me be. I strolled along the narrow alleys leading down to the seashore and out onto the pier. And there she was – moored, as always, with her bowsprit pointing westward. Her name (at the time) was inscribed on the stern with golden letters: *Kimbeth*.

As I had not seen anyone onboard for several months, I did not notice the short, sturdy man sitting on the wheelhouse staircase. Like so many times before, I just stood there, in awe, analysing every little detail of her rigging and the slender yet buoyant hull.

"Well, she's really something to look at, isn't she ...?"

The unmistakable Finland-Swedish accent made me jump as I did not know where the voice was coming from. He was sitting halfway behind the mizzen mast, partly hidden in the shadow. A bit embarrassed and nervous, I replied:

"Yes, indeed, she is... really something..."

"That's good to hear!" This was followed by a hoarse laughter, and before I could react, he continued:

"I've seen you sneak around here like a thief... Are you planning on stealing something, or do you just want to come aboard for a look around?" I nodded hastily and mumbled:

"Yes please, I'd like that very much!"

While I climbed onboard, he remained on the staircase with a toothpick in the corner of his mouth.

"You see, I dislike people in general, but especially those who sneak around my living quarters without stating their business. Those are the kind of people I dislike the most...!"

He removed his greasy leather cap briefly to scratch the top of his head, and continued:

"But you look harmless enough, and if you wanted to steal something you would have tried to already, right?"

"Yeah...I suppose I would have..." Once more realising how stupid my answer sounded.

He laughed again, more of a snort this time, shook his head, and started showing me around.

I found myself in a world of yesterday, on a subtle journey into days long past. There was an abundance of stays and halyards, belaying pins, and blocks of all sizes as well as a small cargo hatch, a wheelhouse with the captain's cabin and the forward hatch leading down to the crews' quarters. By the midship, there was an old-fashioned bilge pump and at the inside end of the bow sprit a mighty anchor winch. Two heavy anchors were resting on each bow.

The ship moved indolently in the light swell, letting out a creaking sound with each wave. A scent of old tar and diesel enclosed this buccaneer ship of my dreams, exuding an air of adventure. With devotion, my senses imbibed every detail, every word, as he guided me from bow to stern. I suddenly realised that he was thoroughly enjoying having a potential apprentice onboard, as he was not showing any sign of hostility or disapproval. I could feel that this was the beginning of a lifelong friendship.

In a somewhat hardy but lenient way, he embraced this daydreaming young man, and taught him how to handle a sailing ship. At any time, come rain or shine, he would knock on my door and say:

"Come on now, let's take her out for a spin…"

Aloft!
(Photo Bo Nilsson)

"A spin" could mean anything from a couple of hours to a couple of days.

And I was carefully instructed, ranging all the way from the very basics. Like how to start the old semi-diesel, how to cast off and land safely, the propellers impact when manoeuvring tight spots, and how to navigate open seas and hazardous, shallow waters. In which order to hoist the heavy sails and how much canvas to carry in strong winds. The winding mysteries of the Radio Direction Finder kept me busy studying for quite a while. Not to forget the important task of watering the compass rose.

The villagers had something new to discuss during their coffee break, as they now and then could see the old ship cruising Öresund. During endless hours in the wheelhouse, I absorbed his knowledge of a whole life at sea. But he never told me about his undertakings on the Irish Sea, or any other dark secrets, such as smuggling in the Finnish archipelago. This was until we anchored in Denmark one stormy night, when he provided thorough instructions on how to sink cans of liquor into the ocean by attaching them to salt sacs, in case the coast guard would turn up out of the blue. The following day, when the salt had melted, the cans would resurface and could be brought back onto the ship.

At last, the day had come for me to set out on my trip to Tahiti. On a sunny morning in September, I left home and did not return until the following spring, only to find *Kimbeth* had been sold! I had planned to continue my sailing with Pekka, conquer the high seas, maybe take on a North Sea crossing! I soon discovered that she had been sold to two Americans, Curt, and Lee, as they had given Pekka an offer he could not refuse. The plans they had for the old ship made some people dream of distant shores and far away exotic places, while others tried to get the authorities to "stop this madness". I was one of the dreamers, of course.

What they had in mind was to give the old lady a thorough overhaul in the summer months to come and set sail for America in the fall. The plan was to follow the old Viking routes; Norway, Faroes, Iceland, South Greenland, Newfoundland, and onwards to the Saint Lawrence River, across Ontario, Erie, Huron, and finally to Lake Michigan, Chicago, where she was to participate in various PR events and do charter trips for tourists.

To honour this challenge, she was renamed: *Spirit of Chicago*. Changing the name of a ship is, by many old sea dogs, considered to be bad luck. Something which may have contributed to the unfortunate events that followed.

With emphasis, my mother was opposed to the mere thought of me crossing the North Atlantic in a sixty-five-year-old sailing ship.

In between my chores onboard, I spent the summer convincing her of the seaworthiness of *Spirit of Chicago*.

The following logbook describes the events that occurred onboard the Baltic Trader *"Spirit of Chicago"* during the late summer of 1971.

July 25

The onboard crew (apart from myself, sailmaker, and engineer) include Curt (captain) and Curt junior, Lee (navigator), Bert (carpenter), Bruce (cook), and Paul (able seaman).

Bruce and Paul will not be with us all the way, they are on leave from the military and must return to Germany in a few days.

The last pieces of equipment were stored onBertard today, a life raft from SAS and a variety of canned food. We are still lacking extra sails. The old ones will not last the entire trip.

In fear of the North Atlantic autumn storms, and in lack of time, we have decided to keep a lookout for used sails on our way to the first stop: Bergen, Norway. We will just have to trust the old semi-diesel. It is infallible.

July 28

Our money for the trip arrived today; 5000 Swedish crowns. The atmosphere onBertard, having been somewhat tense for a while now due to all the critique and irony from the media, has lightened up! We will heave anchor tomorrow!

A grand voyage lies ahead: Viken to Chicago!

At rest in the harbor of Viken
(Photo unknown)

July 29

Damp heat today and thunder in the distance. Febrile preparations all day and spectators started arriving late afternoon – friends, relatives, and a whole lot of curious villagers. At 7:30 p.m., a final goodbye to everyone and then we cast off. Hoorays and applauses echoed across the harbor as we gently left the quay and set course north to Kattegat. Hoisted mainsail and mizzen, which are filling nicely in the light breeze from south-west. The last lighthouse disappeared as a sea mist rolled in. Had a couple of hours of restless sleep and went on watch with Bert at midnight. Sounding the foghorn every other minute. Ghostlike surroundings.

Suddenly, a bright light appeared on starboard bow, getting closer at high speed. It was a huge ferry, heading straight towards us, apparently, they had not seen us on their radar nor heard our foghorn! We made a sharp port turn and got clear of the ferry by 20 meters...

4:00 a.m., went to bed shaken. Woke up to a sunny day. Caught our first fish, mackerel for dinner today! Twelve-volt system not working right. In the evening pouring rain. Deck is leaking in several places.

July 30

Lowered the dinghy for filming. Must pump regularly. Grey and misty afternoon. Wind increasing from south-west. Late in the afternoon, land in sight: the Norwegian coastline. Decided to dock in Kristiansand for Bruce and Paul to disembark and buy some pastries. Wind steadily increasing. I am ordered to lower the mainsail, but a line has gotten stuck. The captain shouts at me to shut of the engine, five minutes later he orders me to start it up again...

It is a dark night, and something is wrong with the rudder. At seven knots speed, we are heading straight towards some rocks. I manage to find out what is wrong with the rudder and got the mainsail down. 8:30 p.m., mooring in Kristiansand.

Most of the crew
(Photo unknown)

July 31

Leaving Kristiansand in high seas. I started to get seasick, and the day becomes a long nightmare, both me and the captain spending the day in our bunks.

I am trying every trick in the book to get better, but it is just getting worse. The nausea makes me weak and dangerously passive. Not much wind, but the swell makes our ship roll like crazy. Everything not tied down properly breaks loose and becomes life threatening projectiles.

August 1

It is about 10:00 a.m., we are approaching the small village of Borhaug on the Norwegian south coast. Passed two rusty wrecks. We entered the small port to ask around for some used sails. Crew rested all day.

August 2

Slept better last night and woke up from the smell of bacon and eggs. Had breakfast together, all of us. Enjoying the still and resting ship. Spending the day buying more essential equipment and provisions. People from the village, of which a number of them turned out to be Americans (!), visits us during the day. We got a hold of a couple of good foresails to replace the old ones. Trimming the rig, which has not been done in years.

A small boatyard at the far end of the bay is in the process of building a new sixty-feet trawler. Three elderly gentlemen are doing the job. Watched two of them for an hour – driving nails, fastening planks with unbelievable precision, using huge sledgehammers.

In the evening, we visited the local pub and enjoyed the fabulous Norwegian beer.

Life returning to weary sailors…

August 3

Getting ready to cast off in the forenoon. Went down into the engine room to prepare for starting the main engine; pump up some fuel, heat the bulb on the cylinder top, check for oil in the lubricator, and lever the heavy flywheel into the right position. Last step, pushing the compressed air lever to push the piston down to start.

I got thrown backwards and hit my head on the bulkhead. The explosion was powerful and turned the cramped engine room into a deadly trap. Soot, parts of metal, and hot fuel filled the air like a blinding fog. Bleeding from multiple face wounds, I managed to crawl back on deck. Captain Curt ran around yelling about my incompetence as an engineer. Lee tended to my injuries, luckily mostly superficial cuts, and bruises. No fire had broken out and, half an hour later, the engine room was fully ventilated. While inspecting the damage, I found that the solid top of the huge cast iron muffler had cracked, leaving a gap of approximately one centimetre. Only one series of events could have caused this; someone had already pumped fuel into the cylinder before I did. The excess fuel ignited when sprayed into the muffler, causing the explosion. My suspicions turned to the captain's young son, who had a habit of exploring and touching things he was not supposed to. I was the only one allowed to care for the engine – starting it, maintaining it, and repairing it. I discreetly revealed my thoughts to Bert and Lee but was overheard by Curt. He got furious, saying we "had no right to accuse his son of anything!" His reaction made the rest of us wonder about him, and his state of mind.

Starting the hot bulb
(Photo unknown)

A few hours later, I managed to make the necessary repairs. Unable to weld, I used a special compound that, when hardened, could withstand high temperatures and moderate pressure.

Eventually, we were on our way again, barely making it out of the narrow harbor entrance, head against an extreme swell that caused turmoil onboard. Spare timber and barrels got loose and threatened to destroy everything in its way. Hoisting the sails did not do much to limit the heeling, there just was not enough wind to stabilise the ship in the heavy seas. With our lives at stake, we managed to secure the spars and clear the deck.

Today I could not help wondering what made our captain leave port in conditions like these. It seems impossible to reason with him as soon as a crisis occurs. When confronted with a problem, he responds with a threat, as if he has been insulted. Lee, on the contrary, keeps calm all the time, and we get to know each other more and more every day. It feels like we are on the same wavelength and know what must be done. Bert does not seem to worry much about anything. He is an excellent carpenter but has never been out at sea before. Curt junior is polite and wants to pull his weight onboard but follows his father wherever he goes.

Everything is not okay with the engine. It seems to lose power every now and then, and we are making slow headway. Quite depressing. After having viewed the same shoreline for several hours, suffering from seasickness, my mood hit rock bottom. The ship should be making better speed while making use of the motor and having all sails up.

Curt stayed in his cabin, refusing to speak to anyone except for his one brief statement about the current being too strong.

Then it struck me – the obvious answer. I felt a rush of excitement as I tumbled down into the engine room. I looked at the flywheel, shook my head and could not keep myself from laughing. Of course, it must have happened when we seemed to lose power. The engine slowed down to the point where it almost stopped, changed, and rerouted into moving... backwards. We were reversing our way across the sea...

With a swift pull on the starter valve, I made it reroute again (into moving forwards, this time...). Within a minute, we were doing a full five knots again! The captain appeared, glared at me, and ordered me and Bert to take a double watch the coming night, between 12:00 and 6:00 a.m.

It felt like we, or at least I, was being punished.

Still seasick, but being at the helm, I can endure it. And it will get better.

August 4

Awoke at noon. Beautiful day with a steady breeze. Course set straight for Stavanger, which came into sight around 4:00 p.m. We were approaching the first fjord. An argument arose between Curt and Lee concerning our current position. Curt ordered us to set course for the closest entrance of the fjord, not far from Kvitsöy. Getting too close to the wind caused a drift towards some gruesome cliffs. On starboard bow, we could see the sharp cliffs approaching. All we had to do to clear it was to steer leeward. Bert tried to talk Curt into altering the course, only resulting in a frightening reply:

"If you don't keep your mouth shut, I'm personally gonna throw you overboard!"

Steadily, we got closer to what may very well have been our total shipwreck, 25 meters, 10 meters... A collision seemed inevitable, and I ran down to get some life jackets. And then, by divine providence, at the very last second, Curt turned the wheel, and we cleared it by a few meters. It was only then that I noticed several small fishing boats had arrived at the scene, as the locals assumed we were lost and had to be rescued.

I managed to convince them that we were all right and they turned to port, bewildered.

For the first time in my life, I experienced the beautiful Norwegian fjords, late summer green with small red farmhouses clinging to the hillsides. Seagulls tracking tar brown trawlers making port, heavily loaded with a day's catch of mackerel and herring. All of them bound for small fish factories, waiting to ennoble the blessings of the sea. Scents of tar, fish, and the hillside woodlands reached us as we continued on a northerly course.

Now that the situation had calmed down, Curt prepared and served a tasty dinner of fried mackerel, potatoes, and chilled beer on the cargo hatch. Darkness approached, and a rainy haze swept in from the North Sea. We were about to set a new course when the visibility got lowered to somewhere around 20 meters. Sea lane markings and light houses were invisible in the thickening fog. Now we were completely dependent on the compass, but nothing made sense. The compass rose kept turning back and forth as if it had been tossed into a room filled with iron ore. Three possible explanations came to mind: the compass was out of order, there was a huge wreck on the seabed, or there was a presence of iron ore in the surrounding mountains. Since the charts did not show any wrecks or notifications of iron, we assumed there was something wrong with the compass. The northerly wind picked up when me and Bert went on watch at midnight. Keeping in the middle of the fjord would ensure that we would not collide with anything. The south-flowing current increased in force quickly, and it became almost impossible to keep the ship moving against the wind, meaning we did not make any headway, whatsoever. Occasionally, lights could be seen from land and, far away, we could spot a glow coming from a smaller town. Straight out on starboard, a foaming surf. At 4:00 a.m. we woke the captain up, and he ordered us to turn due south. Making good speed with the current, we reached the town of Koppervik an hour later. I climbed out onto the bowsprit and acted as lookout when, suddenly, a small cargo ship appeared out of the dark. It signalled five times for us to give way. Curt at the helm would not hear of it and refused to change course. The cargo freighter, heavily loaded, was obviously not able to make any swift turns. A collision was imminent and I, along with the rest of the crew, prepared to jump overboard. With a marginal of maybe 40 meters, the cargo ship managed to turn just enough to avoid collision. As they passed, their crew gave us the finger and shook their fists...

Finally, we were ready to moor along the quay of Koppervik. Curt steered, bow first, into the quay and ordered me to jump three meters ashore with a line. I humbly tried to explain how we could use one line and the ships own movement to get alongside. We came close enough for me to get a line ashore, and I gave sign to Curt at the helm to back up gently, thus getting us alongside.

He leaned out of the wheelhouse and yelled at me:

"Don't you lecture me you shithead, just pull the ship in!" He was foaming at the mouth with rage, and Lee had to stop him from physically attacking me.

"And as for the rest of you, leave him do it by himself... The so-called seaman needs to learn a thing or two..." He continued his screaming, accusing us of sabotaging the whole expedition, and disappeared below deck.

So, I "pulled" the ship alongside and decided to ignore my impulse to grab my knapsack and leave immediately. Shortly after, Lee, Bert, and I gathered by the anchor capstan to talk things over and try to come up with a solution; apparently, our captain was losing his mind and exposing us all to danger. Was it even possible to continue this voyage? Bert produced the idea to knock Curt down, lock him up, and not release him until we were far out at sea.

Lee shook his head slowly.

"If we were to do that, I can tell you that we will never be able to let him out again. I've known Curt long enough to know that he's a dangerous son of a bitch. The way I've seen him act, as soon as things gets a little tough, I'm sure he would kill us all – except junior, of course..." He went on, almost whispering:

"Actually, I have never seen him like this... he's totally out of control..."

We ceased talking as we saw Curt on deck, approaching us. My heart was beating with fear, and I was prepared for just about anything. I could see Lee clenching his fists.

"Hi boys! How about a late-night sandwich? And maybe a glass of aquavit. I've set the galley below. We could sure use it after such a long day!"

So, again, Curt has strangely transformed. In an instant, he turned from Mr Hyde into Dr. Jekyll, as if nothing had happened. Once again, he had turned into the merry, wannabe deep sea sailor.

We exchanged glances and silently agreed on waiting until tomorrow to agree on a final decision.

Tonight, I realised we would never get to cross the Atlantic, not with Curt onboard.

August 5

Seems like we are staying in Koppervik for the weekend. Curt summoned a ship meeting this morning. His better self had reached the same conclusion as the rest of us last night. Following a long discussion, we all agreed to put an end to this venture, sail our ship to Bergen, and sell her or lay her up for the winter.

Bert gave Curt a heavy scolding, calling him an irresponsible, ignorant mother fucker. Afterwards, Bert told me he is afraid of going to sleep since he is convinced Curt is totally capable of killing him with his Bowie knife, should he fall asleep.

I think he is exaggerating, but I am finding it difficult to relax.

August 6

Sunday. The atmosphere has lightened up slightly, although it is still a bit taciturn. All day, I have been trying to think of what to do. Stay on, heading towards Bergen, or leave right here in Koppervik. Talked to Lee about it, and he asked me to stay. We are developing a deep friendship after everything that we have experienced during this short period of time, and I have decided to remain for the rest of the trip.

August 7

At 9:00 a.m., we released the moorings and set course for Bergen. Our excellent Walker patent log had been torn off, leaving us with no ability to determine speed and distance. I think we are making three knots, solely supported by the engine. No sails set. After four hours we were closing in on the city of Haugesund but had to fight the current for another hour and a half before being able to dock.

August 8

Seems like we are not going any further. Curt and Lee have decided to turn around and sail back to Viken. Perhaps to sell *Spirit of Chicago* to a museum.

Thus, we are at the end of the Atlantic crossing. But I feel okay anyway. I have learned a lot and got a friend for life in Lee.

August 9

Slept all day. We have decided to heave anchor tomorrow. The ship's carpenter Bert is signing off. He said that he could not stand the shame of returning so soon. He will try to get onboard a cargo ship headed for the US.

August 10

Said goodbye to Bert. Going with the current now, we are making good speed, heading south.

Only four of us left onboard: Curt, Curt junior, Lee, and I. Just hoping the weather Gods favour us on this journey back home. I cannot rid myself of an uneasy feeling of looming danger. But I feel confident that the two of us, Lee, and myself, can manage to get home safely together. Lee has told me to stay out of the way if Curt becomes violent again. It is a calm night that we pass the Reef of Jären. Our captain sits on the anchor capstan, doing nothing, not uttering a word. Curt junior has made his own hideout in the foc'sle, reading comic strips.

Lee Broske, friend, adventurer, navigator
(Photo: Unknown)

August 11

It is my birthday today! Turning 18, I am getting old... Lee gave me a birthday cake that he bought in Haugesund. Curt and his son have locked themselves in the aft cabin, refusing to talk to us. Lee and I take turns at the wheel and, in the increasing north-west wind, the both of us need to lash the helm from time to time in order to tighten the mainsail sheet. Lee has seemed very serious all day, and we have not talked much. As the night was closing in, he turned to me and said:

"Birger, I don't know this for sure, but I have a strong feeling that Curt may be planning something... foolish... or dangerous. The one of us that is not steering must sleep on the cargo hatch, ready to act, just in case." After a short pause, he looked me in the eyes and continued:

"Whatever happens, Birger, you must promise to do exactly as I say… It's very important!" I could not mistake the sincerity in his voice and nodded.

In the evening, we will reach Lindesnes and plot a course for Skagen, Denmark. The compass seems to be okay now. The barometer is falling, and it looks like it will rain. The wind has shifted for south-west and started increasing as I fell asleep on the cargo hatch.

August 12

Woke up from the sound of the foghorn and someone shouting. As I looked up, I could see the stern of a trawler disappearing in the haze. Lee tells me that Curt suddenly appeared from his cabin and grabbed the wheel without a word, intentionally steered close to the trawler, left the helm, and vanished into his cabin again. I decided to stay awake.

Our ship was gracefully moving this morning, and we are making good distance. Skagen cannot be far now. Later on, the day got gloomy, the wind abated and seemed to come from every direction at once. Lee and I have been sharing our life stories. He told me about his canoeing adventures and his friends among the Sioux Indians. And we have been singing songs. His melodic voice filled the crampy wheelhouse with melancholic French-Canadian canoe songs, and I taught him one of my favourite sea songs.

August 13

Increasing winds today and a lot of rain. At dawn, we have yet to target Skagen. Something is very wrong! We have probably drifted north-east. Later on, this morning, we spotted a shoreline; Danish or Swedish? After a couple of hours, we identified it as Hållö on the Swedish west coast. There is a noticeable north-flowing current and the engine is failing again, with irregular rpm. I suggested to Curt that we head for my home island of Musö and their shipyard with the best of aid due to its owner, Albert. It would not be too much of a detour. Curt told me to shut up.

Making very slow headway south, going along the coast. Weather is clearing up.

August 14

Warm sun today, we got a chance to dry our clothes. Around 10:00 a.m., we saw the fortress of Marstrand. Passing Gothenburg, Tistlarna, and Kungsbacka. Coast guards escorted us for a while as we were passing Gothenburg. They were taking pictures. Fair play, the old ship is beautiful with all its sails up! They got closer and warned us about a storm approaching from the west. The coming hours were going to involve some serious sailing. Curt came out of his dungeon and pompously stated:

"Well, since we failed to get to Chicago, we might as well see what this old lady is made of! Just keep the sails up!" And then he was gone...

In the late afternoon, the wind shifted to straight westerly, rapidly increasing. Dusk came, and we made good speed. But she is taking in a lot of water.

August 15

By midnight, the lee railing was almost constantly under water. Lee and I are taking turns at the bilge pump. Just to stay awake, we ate meat soup out of the can and ryebread with salty sausages. At 3:00 a.m., we reefed the main gaff sail. It is getting harder and harder to keep her on course. *Spirit of Chicago* is rushing forwards in the night, like a young stallion across the stormy seas. I do not know what distance we are making, but probably around ten knots. Mighty seas are breaking over her bows and we are soaking wet. The windward rigging is stretched to its limit and the sails are stiff as boards. A doomsday feeling accompanies us through the night.

With a loud bang, the jib sheet snapped. The sail fluttered an insane amount, and the heavy sheet block swept back and forth with deadly fury.

I am crawling along the deck, constantly flushed with water, soaking wet despite my oilskins. With the use of a rope snare, I finally managed to catch the block and get a new rope in place. As I was reaching for my knife to cut the snare, the block flicked and hit me in the face. The blow threw me backwards, sliding in water along the deck, all the way to the wheelhouse. I was close to fainting and could feel the taste of blood in my mouth. I caught a glimpse of Lee's face in the wheelhouse, but he did not see what happened. He had his hands full keeping the ship on course. Time after time, I am almost flushed overboard, but saved by holding on to the bilge pump handle. I knew it would not come off, since I had secured it with a rusty nail... The blow seemed to have drained all my strength and, with every heeling of the ship, my muscles grew more and more numb. I swallowed a lot of seawater, and what was left of my consciousness was working overtime to try and heave myself over to the windward railing into safety. For a moment, I passed out, but still felt aware of the sensation of being lifted. Lee had noticed what was going on at last. He secured the helm and dragged me into the wheelhouse.

"Jesus... you look awful!" Lee returned to wrestling with the wheel. The ship sheered downwind, and we were not far from a devastating jibe.

"How do you feel? Your face seems to have stopped bleeding, but I could swear someone has just equipped it with a huge Falu sausage..."

It hurt when I laughed at the way he pronounced Falu sausage in Swedish.

I made an averting gesture towards the door to the captain's cabin. Lee shook his head:

"I've been close to kicking down the door, but he won't open it. It makes me wonder if they're dead…"

Amidst my weariness, I could feel a fierce anger. Goddamn moron! He just does not give a shit about us! If he had showed up, none of this would have happened!

"I couldn't care less," I mumbled. "God help us to avoid ever sailing with a 'captain' like that again."

In the dark, we passed Fladen, Varberg, Falkenberg and, as dawn arrived, we were just outside Tylösand. The rising sun dyed the skies, the storm chasing red clouds. I came to think of the old saying:

> *Red skies at night, sailors delight,*
> *Red skies in the morning, sailors warning*

At first, the wind seemed to abate a bit, but now it has returned with even more furiousness.

The leeward stays are limply dangling, but the starboard lanyards could snap at any moment. I wonder how much she can take.

We have maintained a safe and straight course towards Halland's Väderö, just to steer clear of the Cape of Kullen. We have lost some speed but gained necessary height. If nothing breaks, we ought to make port by tonight.

Without a sound, Curt appeared behind us.

"I can see that you two gentlemen have disobeyed my direct orders!" He had a triumphant tone, as he could now confirm our disloyalty. Lee restrained himself and politely answered:

"We must keep this course if we are to steer clear of Cape Kullen…"

Curt slammed his fist on the chart table, it cracked and hurled an open can of meat soup all over the radio direction finder.

"Not a fucking word out of you two again, or I swear you won't make it home alive!"

67

In my mental mist, I realised that Lee is currently evaluating the situation. I am far too young and inexperienced for all of this, but I know for a fact Lee is fully capable of taking care of Curt, should he pull his knife out.

Lee glanced at me and, without uttering a word, we agreed; let the raving maniac decide…

Curt junior appeared in the doorway, white faced and shivering uncontrollably. My heart ached when I saw him.

"Steer downwind and straight for the cape!"

Curt's words were filled with underlying threats, and I eased off on the helm, fully aware that we will never be able to round the cape without having to tack our way out again. Curt pushed me away from the helm and yelled:

"Take down the mainsail!" As Lee and I were wrestling with the big sail, we could agree on one thing: we have ruined our last chance to beat against the wind… Soon after, Carl seemed to have come to the same conclusion and steered straight towards the city of Halmstad. His sudden change of course made the mizzen sail gybe which cracked the boom. We secured the mizzen with ropes and the ship rushed downwind into the dead-end bay of Laholmsbukten.

Curt roared from the wheelhouse:

"Birger, get your ass down to the engine room and start the engine!"

We turned off the motor just outside Gothenburg as our rpm was decreasing. Maybe it could help us make it into port. Maybe.

Since it was too dangerous to contradict the raving maniac, I went down and got the motor running. But that was it. It was running, but only idling. As soon as I increased the regulator, it choked and went back to idling. If I had had a little more experience of these fantastic hot-bulb engines, I would have known what was wrong: water in the fuel… easily fixed.

With no chance of turning back, our old, beautiful ship was rushing to its own, inevitable destruction. And Curt's confused orders kept coming:

"Take down the mizzen sail!"

Without the mizzen we would completely lose our manoeuvrability. But with only the jib and outer jib, we still had a rapidly diminishing chance to make port in the town of Halmstad.

I pleaded to Curt to steer upwind in order to get the mizzen down. He let go of the helm, rushed out, knife in hand, made a threatening pass at Lee, climbed up the mizzen mast, and started to cut down the sail. With no one at the helm, the ship turned sideways against the wind and rolled furiously. On his way down the mast, he cut all the halyards for the gaff boom, and slashed the sail witch crashed down on deck.

"That's the way to take down a sail!" His words were almost undistinguishable in the storm and, with insanity glowing in his eyes, he roared his last order:

"Get the emergency transmitter that we borrowed from SAS and get the coast guards out here! I want them to get junior!" Lee went to get life jackets and I found the transmitter. The situation was horribly unreal. The only thing on my mind was to try to survive, get ashore, and alienate myself from this madman as soon as possible. But if Curt kept this course, we would not make it. The ship would become stranded in the shallow waters, masts snapped, exposing all of us to a certain death by a falling rig or drowning.

Lee patiently tried to make Curt come to his senses but gave up and started pumping. The transmitter seemed to be working as it should, but my repeatedly transmitted words ("Mayday, mayday") remained unheard. Ängelholm airport was not too far away, and this device was made to be used in the middle of the Atlantic to all emergency airplane channels!

"S/V Spirit of Chicago in distress, Bay of Laholm, need immediate assistance…"

Swedish pilot cutter
(Photo unknown)

I went on for quite a while but received no answer. I gave up and joined Lee by the anchor capstan. We awaited the end. The storm, now reaching its peak, with salty foam filling the air, turning the shallow waters into an inferno. I shouted in Lee's ear:

"At the first sign of the ship hitting the bottom, we jump overboard at windward!" He nodded and stuck a waterfilled smoking pipe into his mouth.

"We must take junior with us too! But whatever you do, keep away from Curt!"

When the next breaking wave hit us, he managed to hold on to the pipe... I looked at him, with his sou'wester foiled back, like a half-peeled orange, water running from his pipe and beard. I burst into a hysterical laughter and shouted:

"Have you looked in the mirror lately...?"

All the tension and hardships we had been through lately, not to mention the lack of sleep, overwhelmed us at that very moment, and as the shore rapidly approached us, we just kept laughing. All hope was lost. Helplessly, we drifted past the harbor inlet. I tried to mentally prepare myself for what was to come, as the waters grew more and more shallow. At least we would have an opportunity to surf in our life jackets. But I did not want to stay in harm's way of the falling rig that, most likely, would come crashing down as the ship hit the seabed.

Thankfully, at the very last moment, salvation came in the form of the Halmstad Pilots. They had observed our extremely bad seamanship and came charging to our rescue. They closed in on the port side and, before we knew it, a throwing line landed on our bow. Lee quickly grabbed it and, together, we hauled in the thick towing line, securing it around the main mast. Curt's face showed up in the wheelhouse window. He was gesticulating fiercely, but we ignored him and gave sign to the Pilot to start towing.

Half an hour later, we were safely moored in the town of Halmstad. I, once more on this trip, contemplated leaving for the train station right there and then. But Lee sat down with me, and, on the quayside, we observed our battered, floating home of the last few weeks. Worn down she was, indeed, the old lady. However, despite her old age, she was surprisingly seaworthy. Something she had proved last night. She had done well in the high seas and did not take in more water than was easily bilged out. With new sails and perhaps a somewhat more skilled engineer, she could cross many open seas. Except for the North Atlantic in the fall. And with another captain.

Now that we had the ability to speak without screaming, somehow, we ran out of words. There just was not anything more to say. We had failed but survived, gaining experiences for life. To put it mildly.

Curt came walking towards us, and we both wondered if it was as Doctor Jekyll or Mr Hyde. We could have spared ourselves the speculation, Doctor Jekyll smiled and said:

"How about a juicy steak now, boys! There's a nice restaurant just across the river!"

Epilogue

A small consortium consisting of my American friends, Pekka, and I bought the *Spirit of Chicago* for 5000 crowns. Two weeks later, we sold her at a profit to two families who were planning on sailing her to the east coast (and we were planning on using the profits for another venture). The following spring, they left Halmstad for their new home port. Unfortunately, they paid no attention to my instructions concerning the engine and keeping an eye on the condensation in the fuel tank. Failing to tack their way out of the Bay of Laholm, they ran aground on the rocky shallows of Tylösand. A week later, she was wrecked by a gale. All that is left of her, parts of the hull and the hot bulb engine, are resting peacefully among the seaweed, mussels, and barnacles.

Lee and I became friends for life.

*The poem of Don Blanding was rewritten by Lee Broske,
September 1971and given to me as a preface in the
book "American Practical Navigator"
that he gave me as a farewell gift.

Chicago
May 14, 1973

To Whom it may concern:

Please let it be known that one - Mister Birger Sjöberg - is in my opinion, well qualified to be a deckhand, above or below decks on any sailing or engine craft sailing on the high seas.

In the summer months of 1971, Mr. Sjöberg was a crew-member on the "Spirit of Chicago" (Kimbeth) of Viken Sweden.

He is well capable in the handling of all miscellaneous ship work and is not too proud to do the most menial of ships tasks.

He is a crew member that would do any ship or ships Master, a credit.

Sincerely and Yours in Respect.

Mr. L. D. Broske (Captain G.L.W.W.)
Rainbow Chaiser
Register Chicago H.S.C.P.D.

THE BRIG UNICORN

"Ships are the nearest things to dreams that hands have ever made, for somewhere deep in their oaken hearts the soul of a song is laid."

Robert N. Rose

The Unicorn arriving in New York
(Photo unknown)

Built in 1947 in Borgå, Finland, from pine softwood. Originally rigged as a schooner, shipping sand in the archipelago of Finland. Her original name was *Lyra of Borgå* Overall length: 28.5 meters. Beam: 7.4 meters.

Purchased by five part-owners and, during the following two years, rerigged based on records from the brig *Adolph and Laura*, built in 1867. Total sail area: 400 square meters, distributed on fifteen sails. Main engine: GM Diesel 153 horse powers.

Materializing a dream

The very same autumn that Spirit of Chicago got new owners (and got shipwrecked), a new project got started. The American friends that I met in the US, Jacob and his wife Betty, Pekka the Finn, my mate Olaf, and I embarked on the remarkable venture to transform an old sand freighter into a sailing brig. For that purpose, we bought the ship *Lyra* in Sibbo, Finland, and sailed her home to Viken, Sweden. Her new name: *Unicorn*. The plan was to establish a foundation called "Windjammer Society", recruit more motivated people to join us, rerig, and equip the ship for sailing the deep blue seas.

Our first task was to, by hand, unload twenty tons of sand ballast and make some vital improvements on the hull. In February, we went to a nearby forest and bought all the necessary timber for the rigg, such as masts and spars, all of them ring-barked to dry evenly. Also, a considerable amount of larch wood was purchased to make new cargo hatches. A fair number of sleepless nights were spent trying to get it all together, the material, time schedules and, of course, the money. The raw materials needed for this project were expensive already, due to their unprocessed state. But somehow this project, from the very beginning, was permeated by an astonishing air of ingenuity and skills of how to acquire things with persuasion and actions bordering on theft but designated as "loans". Jacob revealed skills of persuasiveness that were beyond comprehension and ensured large numbers of equipment – for free...

Soon enough, the work force consisted of a colourful bunch of people from all over the world with unique talents, often usable skills, and unconventional methods of acquiring necessary material.

The ship as we found her
(Photo P. Tarvas)

Jacob, by all of us considered to be the "Primus Motor", turned out to be the most charming, deceitful con-artist I have ever come across. His talents can hardly be described in words but must be experienced. Because of them, he succeeded in convincing his wife Betty's guardian to release her entire fortune in advance. A handy, initial contribution of 1,5 million dollars to this challenging project.

Betty basically could be described as a kind and emphatic person, always trying her best to tackle the different tasks bestowed upon her. However, her personality harboured the firm belief that, in order to keep a cheerful atmosphere onboard, she had to try to seduce every male crew member – which is quite amusing in retrospective. With varying success, she would undertake this mission, which often caused palpable tension around the breakfast table. As she was an attractive woman, married to a man who was not really bothered, she was often successful in her efforts. The lucky crew member presently in her favour had to endure lots of taunts and comments.

In the harbor of Viken
(Photo P Tarvas)

Jesus from the Philippines turned out to be a valuable asset since he had a natural talent of shaping masts and spars into perfection. He could handle adzes and planers with professional skill but, unfortunately, he craved smokable substances which had some negative effects on our time schedule.

Eric, a subtle and loveable man, joined us from the US with his wife and three children. He claimed he was being chased around the globe by a malicious prosecutor. We had no reason to doubt his fear, but never really got a grip on why he was on the run either. I can easily stay friends with all kinds of people, but later on Eric and I got into a brawl over a motorcycle that was recklessly offered, to both of us, by Jesus. Unaware of this "dual give-away", I sold the motorcycle several months later for five hundred crowns, as it was broken and had been sitting in my mother's garden, leaking oil, and rusting away.

From that day on, Eric considered me to be hostile and unreliable and would not talk to me.

Olaf, my friend, and travel companion developed his carpenter skills during this project. We stuck together through it all and, in the end, we got conned together as well.

Pekka the Finn's knowledge was essential for the entire venture. He was a master of all kinds of craft and possessed a marvellous ability to solve any technical problem that occurred, regardless of the material needed. His abilities came in handy on an expedition where we "loaned" anchor gear from a stranded Danish trawler, shipwrecked just north of the village of Viken – something which is hopefully now long forgotten by legal authorities.

The wreck looters

At the time, *Unicorn* was moored in Viken harbor, made ready for the trip down to Ystad for rigging and supplementary equipment. One of the challenges was the issue of acquiring a better anchor capstan. The one onboard was ancient, half rotten, and dangerous to use. About a year earlier, a severe storm swept in over the west coast, forcing all seaborn vessels to seek shelter at the nearest port. Every ship made it except for *Mette of Vedbaek*, a Danish trawler. She got stranded just north of the lighthouse of Svinbådan. Fortunately, no lives were lost. The owner removed everything of value, and she was left to perish in the next heavy storm. Some said she was for sale and soon to be towed away, but that never happened.

One item that was not removed by the owner was a huge, modern cast iron anchor capstan. A great piece, just sitting there…

During a dark, moonless February night, a few conspiring crew members gathered in the captain's cabin on *Unicorn*. While the coffee was brewing, Pekka presented a bottle with golden content, but no label.

"I have saved this for a special occasion – one that requires extra strength and nerve… One of my business acquaintances in the Baltic gave it to me…"

The people who had gathered this night would have done anything to get him to reveal something about his doings in the Baltic Sea. But of course, no one tried. Everyone knew it was a useless attempt. He was a man of mystery.

The captain's cabin was roomy and cosy, with its brown wooden panelling and sooty ceiling. A sturdy desk and wall mounted benches occupied most of the space, and another round table was attached to a clever invention which was keeping it levelled. The captain's private toilet was installed in one of the wall mounted benches, hidden underneath a beautifully carved hatch. A kerosene lamp spread a soft light, creating sweeping shadows that moved along with the ship's calm swell. In cups the size of soup bowls, Pekka served coffee which was diluted with at least fifty percent of his golden nectar. From the open portholes a cool, southerly wind helped scatter the tobacco haze, and an air of suspense dominated the cabin as Jacob took the floor:

"Well ladies and gentlemen, tonight's the night, and the outcome is dependent on our full cooperation…" He paused, looked everyone straight in the eye, and continued:

"The longboat is prepped and has most of the equipment onboard. Burger and Olaf will take it to the shoreside of the wreck and meet us at the beach. Pekka, Jesus and I will join you from land in the VW bus and bring the empty barrels. Jan and Staffan will keep a lookout from the beach." Another pause, followed by his characteristic smile:

"Remember, we are only to communicate via light signals! Make sure to rehearse them on your way over there."

At the stroke of eleven thirty, Pekka got up from his chair and proposed a toast:

"Here is to a successful night!"

The old anchor capstan
(Photo Olle Blomqvist)

I do not possess "nerves of steel", which is why my heart was beating fiercely from the mere thought of what we were about to do. Olaf smoked his Camel's and looked like a true wannabe thief, sitting on the canvas cover that was concealing all the hand tools, the welding torch, and bundles of rope. His calm demeanour never ceased to impress me. The old Seagull's outboard motor started on the first try, so we sneaked out of the harbor in the light breeze and set course for Svinbådan lighthouse. Half an hour later, we could discern the dark contours of the wreck, some three hundred meters from the seashore. Using the flashlight, Olaf signalled ashore: two shorts, one long. The response came immediately: one long, two shorts. After mooring alongside the wreck, we unloaded the equipment and, while Olaf remained onboard, I went ashore to pick up the rest of the crew.

The night was pitch black and the deck of *Mette af Vedbaek* had a heavy lean, making all movements cumbersome, which resulted in lots of forceful swearing.

Everyone knew what to do. Silently and well-rehearsed, we covered the foredeck with a canvas cover to eliminate any light that may erupt from the torch. The empty barrels were prepared, tied together with ropes, and moored in the stern, awaiting its heavy load. From an earlier reconnaissance trip, we knew we would have to use a welding torch to loosen the capstan. Pekka got to work, assisted by Jacob while Jesus searched the half-waterfilled engine room for anything else worth "borrowing". Olaf and I had our eyes fixed on the beach, watching out for any warning signals.

An hour went by as the torch blazed on in the background. There were many more bolts to cut than we anticipated, some of them in tricky places, and every now and then we had to put out small fires caused by the torch flame. A cloud of oily smoke surrounded us all the while. I nervously paced back and forth on deck, constantly watching out for police or coast guards, hoping our friends kept a sharp look-out from the beach. By 2.30 a.m., Pekka crawled out from underneath the cover.

"Now we just have to get this monstrosity overboard."

I went ashore to get the rest of the crew, since all of our fourteen arms were needed in order to move the anchor winch to the railing, using crowbars and leavers, and secure it with enough rope to attach it to the empty barrels. So, with a unanimous heave, it went overboard and disappeared into the dark. Fortunately, Pekkas calculations about the buoyancy of four empty oil barrels turned out to be accurate, but just barely... Only two of the barrels were visible above the surface.

As dawn broke, Olaf and I unloaded tools as well as five crewmembers onto the beach and headed back to port, pulling at barely one knot as the capstan was weighing the longboat down to its railings. Mooring right under the bowsprit of *Unicorn,* we climbed onboard for a well-earned breakfast: fried rye bread, fried herring, bacon, and coffee. The capstan was left hidden under water the whole day, for no one to see, but when the evening came, we used the cargo boom to get it up on deck.

From an empty hull to a sailing ship

Later that spring, we cast off and used the motor to get to the town Ystad, situated at the southernmost point of Sweden. At night, just outside Falsterbo reef, we were called upon by the coast guards, who claimed that our lanterns were too weak and could not be seen from a distance. After explaining that they ran on kerosene, the guards shook their heads and took off. My brother Staffan and I had watch, steering due east when we suddenly spotted a sphere-shaped object on starboard bow. As we got closer, there could be no doubt as for what it was. A relic from a dark past, freed from its chains, drifting westward with its deadly horns rolling back and forth. At that time, some twenty-five to thirty years after World War II, they still appeared every now and then. We reported it as soon as we made port in Ystad.

On the slipway
(Photo Olle Blomqvist)

From here on out, an intense period began for everyone onboard, all of us doing our best to get the ship ready for the high seas as the beautiful, smooth sailing ship that it was. Every detail was made by hand. All sorts of fittings, iron reinforcements, bolts, and nails were hand crafted in the boatyard's blacksmith shop. Hundreds of meters of standing galvanized rigging wire were cut, spliced, oiled, and dressed in tarred marling. Eyelets, blocks, and belaying pins were lathed, varnished, and equipped with spliced loops. New hatches were made for the two cargo holds and a thirteen-meter-long bowsprit was put into place.

Down below, eight separate cabins were made and, of course, a functional galley and head (toilet). Slowly, masts and spars were transported from the workshop, oiled, and fitted with all the necessary accoutrements. Each of the two masts consisted of three separate parts, joined together by forged iron fittings. Kilometres of sisal hemp was cut into blocks, except for the lanyards, where we used tarred Russian hemp. The engine room had a total makeover with a new diesel generator, fuel tanks, and a clever, pressurized system for the toilet.

Right below the new inner floor, fifty tons of ballast was placed, with additional space for twenty tons, just in case.

All fifteen sails were ordered from a sail loft in Ireland: nine square sails, three foresails, two staysails and a gaff sail – all made of first-class Navy Flax, which is weaved with cotton and hemp. All of them were lined by hand with tarred hemp rope.

Single 2" block made of oak.
(Photo: the author)

During this period, late summer of -72, two other Finnish sand freighters joined us at the boatyard for a yearly overhaul and repairs. *Marita* was one of them, owned by two gentlemen from Stockholm. It was rerigged back to its original state as a schooner and is, to the best of my knowledge, still sailing in the Baltic to this day. The other one was called *Carita* and owned by a former brothel keeper from Marseilles, Madame Babette. It sailed with a, to say the least, shady crew which consisted of her lover Eskil from Norway (professional thief), her former lover Jean-Jacob (wanted by Interpol for double homicide), her young daughter Michelle, her even younger son Daniel, two Canadians (George and Brad), and an American by the name of Big John.

Madame Babette's ship was constantly struck by bad luck, which probably was due to the motley crew. Eskil and Jean Jacob dwelled in an ongoing competition about who was to be the captain. Like a couple of roosters, they spent their days suspiciously circling each other, without really getting anywhere. Madame Babette was a lady with extensive experience from most parts of life, and she possessed an undeniable air of authority. However, she told me that she was completely dependent on her crew to get back to her hometown of Tabarka, Tunisia. Her reason for buying a ship was to create a steady and safe home for herself and her children. She had given up her former trade and was willing to invest all her savings into building a new life. However, the two antagonists Jean Jacob and Eskil's fighting only got worse and could have ended in bloodshed. Taking the safe way-out, Eskil stole just about all of Madame Babette's savings and disappeared for good.

Jean Jacob, now made captain, stayed onboard a while but departed hastily when he found out that the police were on to him for stabbing two guys to death in Brest. And so, he stole the remainder of Madame Babette's money and took off.

As if this was not bad enough, *Carita* was in a poor state. A lot of woodwork had to be done on the hull and deck. The bow stem seemed to have been attacked by woodpeckers, and the rudder was missing big chunks. Madame was not too worried about such trivial matters, what concerned her the most was the fact that her daughter seemed to be falling in love with George, one of the Canadians. And they did become a couple, committing to marry once they got home to Tabarka.

Her son, eight-year-old Daniel, was of even greater concern since he seemed to be constantly absent-minded and, time after time, got himself into trouble. On two occasions I came to his rescue. The first incident happened during a late afternoon while parts of the crew were caulking the hull and deck. This requires, besides tarred hemp fibre, boiling thick tar. Little Daniel, with his eyes gazing at the setting sun, walked pass the big pot of hot pitch and stuck two of his fingers in it. He had a moment of surprise and disbelief before the pain struck him. I stood right next to him, watching tar and pieces of skin slowly drip down his arm, and decided to make use of some advice I had gotten from Pekka. Hastily, I grabbed Daniel's hand, shoved it into a bucket of linseed oil, and kept it there for about fifteen minutes. Daniel stopped crying almost immediately. Sterile compresses and a bandage finished the job. Two weeks later, his fingers were completely healed. I do not know what medical science has to say about this, but it worked.

The second incident occurred during a Sunday evening. I was sitting in the captain's cabin, studying charts of the Caribbean, when I looked through a porthole and noticed Daniel walking along the quay. I looked down on the charts for a second and, when I looked back up, the boy was gone. Vanished. I rushed out on deck in an instant and called out for him but received no answer. As I reached the railing, I could see his hair floating in between the side of the ship and the concrete quay, barely visible among all the seaweed, pieces of driftwood, and one solitary dead rat. A few seconds later, the ship was pushed by a slow swell, grinding its side onto the concrete. By hanging on to a chain plate with one leg, I managed to reach down just far enough to grab his hair and pull him up to my shoulder, a mere moment before the ship's side hit the quay. He seemed unconscious at first but threw up on my back after a couple seconds. Boy, did he complain about his sore scalp for a long time afterwards.

Provided with heaps of toys, soft drinks, and cinnamon buns, he got tied down in a safe spot in the boatyard, made content by all of the attention he received from us. We developed a clever system where we all took turns watching him.

Madame expressed her gratitude by throwing a party with lamb chops, couscous, and red wine. Moved by our concern and assistance in getting *Carita* under way, she called on Allah's blessing for all of us, wishing us long lives filled with many wives and kids.

Our three big sailing ships docked in the harbor of Ystad, creating a vintage atmosphere of times gone by. There was an echoing sound from adzes, caulking hammers, band saws, and blacksmith hammers mixed with the scent of tar, wood, and linseed oil. Spectators came from all around to experience a glimpse of the past, and we all felt like we were taking part in a once in a lifetime event.

But the magic came to an end around midsummer, as *Marita* was the first to leave for her home port of Stockholm. Shortly after, *Carita* left for a "business trip" to Copenhagen, only to return a week later. Madame went ashore and disappeared for a few days, conducting some business of her own. A brief return and another farewell later, *Carita* set off for the Kiel canal and future adventures. Little did I know that our paths would cross again.

S/V Marita av Borgå
(Photo unknown)

Alone once more, waddling in the late summer winds, *Unicorn* was almost ready to set sail, but a lot of work remained. I was sent out on a fund-raising mission to Stockholm. Against all odds, I managed to make an appointment with a member of the wealthiest family in Sweden, the Wallenbergs. During a full half hour, the patriarch patiently listened to my pleading for sponsor money, served an excellent cup of coffee in porcelain from the Qing dynasty, said "Thanks, but no thanks", bid me adieu, and wished me luck.

I returned to the ship.

The author at the helm
(Photo Olle Blomqvist)

It was unanimously decided that I, for some obscure reason, was to act as the ship's doctor. Jacob performed a long monologue in which he declared the absolute necessity of having someone onboard to perform appendix surgery, remove wood splinters from punctured lungs, and pull-out aching teeth.

At first, I objected fiercely and exposed my total absence of knowledge in those areas, asserting that I had never performed surgery, let alone gotten close to pulling out people's teeth. Due to his masterful skills of persuasion, and with the deceitful acclamation of the rest of the crew, he eventually lured out a trepidatious "Okay" from me.

As a grand finale, he proclaimed:

"And Burger, how hard can it be? Just pay the local hospital a visit and ask them to teach you a thing or two!" He made a brief pause, waiting for the crew to applaud.

"By the way, your father is a doctor, so I bet you already have a head start!"

Again, his ability to make people feel indispensable was undoubtable. Encouraged by the admiration and enthusiasm of the crew, he could not stop himself from continuing:

"We trust you Burger and I know you will not let us down! We must fully trust one another, one hundred percent, at all times. And we will not keep any secrets from one another either. We will stick together and share everything. The five of us started this project, but we will share the fruits of it with everyone onboard – like brothers and sisters!" There was not a dry eye on deck.

The following day, I went to the local hospital and met with the hospital's chief physician, an elderly, stern man with wild, bushy eyebrows. He was busy reading patient journals and seemed to be ignoring me. I humbly explained my wish to practice for a few days and said I just wanted to learn about first aid and whatever else necessary, as I was going to be the onboard doctor of a ship on the high seas.

Without looking up from his papers he said:

"Of course. Report to the ward physician, you can start today. Also, I know your father. I have met him once."

Bewildered, I made my way to the ER to start a week's worth of intensive courses on how to save lives in ways I never could have imagined. After practicing local anaesthesia and learning how to make surgical stiches on a doll, I got to do it for real on a split open scalp, two thumbs, three eyebrows, and the abdomen of an old lady that had just gone through gallbladder surgery. I was also pulling fractures into place, applying plaster on a broken leg, and stopping blood. On the final day, I practiced cardiac massage and artificial breathing.

Confident and proud of my new position onboard, I returned to my carpentry chores, only to get a severe cut on my right thumb the day after on the circle saw. My colleagues at the hospital sewed it back together again, leaving a scar for life.

Masting in progress
(Photo Olle Blomqvist)

Betrayal and departure

August turned into September, and we were all out of funds. Everybody was overworked and exhausted. Not getting under way affected all of us. People grumpily started arguing over trifles and seemed to have lost all enthusiasm. Jacob the patriarch's speeches became more and more desperate and strident in his attempt to make us all work harder and faster. A shadow of suspicion grew larger day by day, mostly aimed towards Pekka and Jacob.

It was on the last night of September that it all came to an end. Olaf and I got into an argument with Pekka about how to make the best of it, how to find a way out of our despair and negative feelings. Olaf said:

"The thing is, we are never doing anything but hard work. What we need to do is get out to sea, if only for a day, just to breath some sea-air!" I could see Pekka begin to clench his fists as Olaf continued:

"It is like we have lost our sense of unity, working together on our own ship… Instead, it feels like we are sweating away on a pile of wood…"

Pekka looked up and the expression on his face sent chills down my spine. I had never seen him like that. When he spoke, his voice was filled with rage:

"I do not give a fuck About what you think or what you want! This is not a goddamn playground! I am here for the sole purpose of guarding my investment, nothing else." He breathed heavily and stared at us with black eyes as his intonation turned scornful:

"You kids do not know anything… do you? No, of course not, but I have got some news for you…" He reached for some papers in the cupboard behind him and said:

"Half of this ship is mine and, so help me God, I will see to it that she is finished, and I will sail her out of this shithole!"

No one said a word, we just looked at each other in silence. Dead silence. A faint sound from the Poland ferry reached us from outside, accompanied by the ever-present creaking of the hull.

"What did you just say Pekka?" I asked, my voice merely a whisper.

"Are you deaf? Do you want me to shout it in your fucking ear!?" His voice was now so full of spitefulness that I got a feeling of being in imminent danger. I cleared my throat:

"But what is this… What do you mean? We are five part-owners! You, me, Olaf, Jacob, and Betty!"

"Bullshit, I have a legal document stating ownership of fifty percent of this ship! The other half belongs to Jacob and Betty."

At a safe distance, he showed us the contract and owner's deed. Olaf leaned his head against the bulkhead and lit a cigarette, his face pale and hands shaking. Inger, my fiancé, joined us.

"What is all the fuzz about?" Pekka showed her the document, leaned back on his chair, and rested his feet on the table. I was speechless, and so was Olaf, but Inger was shaking with fury and her voice was filled with contempt.

"How the hell could you do this, Pekka? It has been agreed upon this whole time; all five of you are part-owners! Equal shares!" Carefully, Pekka stowed the deed away and slowly shook his head.

"You are such a stupid, naive, little girl. Did you really think I would settle for a fifth of the ship? Do you think I am insane or... braindead? Jacob and I have had this agreement ever since we bought the ship in Finland. Since I am the engineer or, if you prefer, the "Master Mind" of all this, I could not settle for less."

He finished the rest of his cold coffee, left the chair, and concluded:

"And if you do not like it, get the hell out of here! You have been fucked, conned, every one of you... You are just useless kids, deadweight... So, take your bullshit dreams and fuck off!" He turned, walked up on deck, jumped ashore, and drove off in the VW bus – and I never saw or heard from him again. It was the turbulent end of what I thought would be a lifelong friendship.

I was devastated.

In a state of total apathy, we stayed below deck, smoking away on Olaf's cigarettes while *Unicorn* moved softly in the evening swell. Her movements, the smell of her, every remote corner of this ship we knew as our home for future adventures on the seven seas – it was all gone now, all turned into ashes.

Slowly we realized, not only that we had been tricked, but that we, in youthful ignorance, had trusted in words. Words and promises between friends, friends already tied together by mutual experiences, made into an unbreakable bond. During almost two years, we had been residing in a well-camouflaged castle in the air. Not in a thousand years could we have foreboded this treason. Jacob' fatherlike and reassuring concern was all we needed. And Pekka, our friend and mentor, our teacher, who gained confidence while doing various crafts onboard...

Epilogue

The morning after, we left. Rumours spread quickly onboard, and chaos broke out at the breakfast table. Everyone became furious and disgusted by how things had turned out, and most of the crew decided to take off, except for a few of the ones that had recently arrived. Jacob, who had spent the night elsewhere, returned just in time to see all of the commotion. I went to meet him and, as soon as he looked me in the eye, he realized what had happened. What had once been top secret was now finally out in the open. By way of cringed excuses, he tried to explain himself and lessen the importance of ownership. But for the first time in our friendship, his words sounded false, deceptive, and confused – his verbiage drained. We dismissed his lame attempts at persuading us to stay, and left *Unicorn* in the frosty September morning.

To heal our emotional wounds, Olof and I went to the island by the Bohuslän archipelago with our girlfriends – penniless, but a bit wiser.

Additional crew signed on and *Unicorn* left Ystad a month later. She arrived in the West Indies in the spring of -73, cruising the islands with cargo and passengers. At one point, she was almost shipwrecked in Grenada, but eventually came out unscathed and sailed to New York. Some years later, she was sold to someone in Fort Lauderdale, Florida, and had a total makeover with lots of brass, varnish, and copper plating. *Unicorn* was featured in the film *Roots* and, later on, in the *Pirates of the Caribbean* films.

The end

In 2010, I came across an article in St. Lucia Times stating that she had been scuttled for insurance. It was never confirmed but would truly be a sad ending for a beautiful ship, resting on the ocean floor outside St. Lucia in the Caribbean.

In a letter from Betty dated October 24, 1975, she wrote:

"...I would never have tried to cheat anyone, we have all been tarnished by Jacob, his lies and deception...I never got paid for my share of the ship, I divorced Jacob and got conned like the rest of you..."

//" ...there will always be ghosts haunting that ship... we will always be there inside the wood and sails, and paint and tar, to remind the world that there once was a beautiful dream that because of lack of trust, greed and lies, could never live..."//

Unicorn as a charter ship in St. Lucia not long
before she was lost forever.
(Photo unknown)

Windjammer SOCIETY
PRO VIE

Letter of Introduktion.

Fack
S-290 17 Everöd
Sweden

tel. 044/23 84 84
0450/102 32
Bg 272-6008

UNICORN January 1973

Herby is certified that MR. BIRGER SJÖBERG of Viken Sweden
has served as a Boatswain and Seaman onboard my ship the brig
"UNICORN" during a period of eleven (11) months.
He has also during this time with great credit participated
in the idealistic task of leading the restoration work onboard
the ship and has shown great capability to colaborate with
other people during severe conditions.

Captain and owner

CHAT BOTTÉ

*"There is, one knows not what sweet mystery about this
sea, whose gently awful stirrings seem to speak of some
hidden soul beneath..."*

Herman Melville

The Irequois catamaran *Chat Botté*
(Photo: the author)

H aving left the brig *Unicorn* in anger and disappointment,
we felt a defiant urge to restore our self-confidence and
somehow find a way to sail the oceans, experience the
vast waterways of the world, and explore distant horizons. Due to
many reasons, my fiancé Ie and I thought and talked a lot about
having the West Indies be our next destination. *Unicorn* would
have brought us there, had things turned out different. Crossing the
Atlantic on a square-rigged ship was the romantic dream that kept

us working so hard, investing mind, body, and all our money into a project governed by greed. As things turned out, we were to make an Atlantic crossing in a vessel which could not be more different.

When World War II ended and people were able to explore the oceans again, many took the opportunity to sail to the West Indies. As a child in the '60s, I heard stories of hazardous endeavours involving old wooden ships who were following the trade winds and heading for the Caribbean (with varying success).

According to rumours, many private yachts left the Canary Islands for Barbados, Grenada, and St. Vincent around new year, after the hurricane season. And many of them needed extra crewmembers. Of course, this was hearsay, but we could not care less. It sounded plausible and was worth an honest try. In February, we got tickets for Tenerife and set off for an unpredictable adventure.

Tenerife is a wonderful place for relaxing, swimming and enjoying the sun, but harboured no private yachts. We were told by a fisherman to go to Gran Canaria instead. There, in the capital Las Palmas, most of the private yachts would gather to prepare for the West Indies. A small airplane took us there the next day, and we got installed in a shabby hotel swarming with cockroaches. But it was cheap.

Early the following morning, we went Atlantic Crossing-hunting. The inner harbor of Las Palmas resembled a huge sewer with a foul stench of oil, rotten seaweed, trash, human excrement, dead rats, and dogs. Four long piers stretched out from the centre of Las Palmas, and we decided to explore the middle one first, since a number of masts could be seen further out. Having strolled just a few meters, we came to a halt, paralyzed. In front of us, moored on the back of a German trawler, was *Carita*! She had a funny small wheelhouse, a clipper bow, and a worn appearance. It just had to be her, no doubt about it. It was the sistership of *Unicorn,* which left Ystad and headed for the Mediterranean. How did she get here? Were our old friends still on the crew?

My girlfriend working the sails on the deck of *Carita*
while the "captain" observes from the foredeck.
(Photo: the author)

We were dizzy with questions as we rushed onboard. And, yes, they were all there: Madame, her kids, the Canadians, two newcomers, and, of course, Jean-Jacob, now wearing a gold-striped captain's hat. On a dark night in Oostende, he had sneaked onboard after evading the police. We had a heart-warming reunion and got the whole story.

During an uneventful passage all the way down to Gibraltar, Madame was persuaded to reconsider her final goal, the town of Tabargah, Tunisia. Her crew unanimously agreed that their life, health, and finances would be better off cruising the Caribbean, doing charter, and shipping cargo among the islands. Understandably, Jean-Jacob eagerly supported this idea, considering his reason for leaving Europe. Madame spent two whole days contemplating in Gibraltar, but ended up not changing her mind, which resulted in a great commotion wherein Madame had to lock herself in her cabin to avoid the angry crew.

Madame's daughter Michelle finally settled the matter. She made it clear that she would rather die than settle in Tabargah. She refused to go anywhere but west. And so, Madame set course for the Canary Islands where they had been moored for two months now.

We immediately signed on and tried to get the ship ready for the trade winds over the duration of three hectic weeks. The engine got an overhaul, as well as the rigging, the sails were repaired, and provisions and equipment were brought onboard. But the flaws of *Carita* were obvious. In retrospect, having been a sailmaker and marine consultant for over fifty years, I must admit that she was in no condition to travel the high seas. Thirty years of neglected maintenance had resulted in too many critical "soft spots", entailing that most of her hull planking needed to be changed. Her sails, made of linen, were in a questionable post-war state and would not have stood against a minor gale.

We kept on working and relaxing at Pepe's Bodega in the evening, enjoying their two-dollar fried chicken. Late at night, we gathered on the foredeck of *Carita* and drank the local rum; Ron Arehucas at one dollar per litre. It did not taste too bad, providing that it had been diluted with a soft drink. Vast consumption, however, could result in a temporary loss of sight. This happened to Bradley, who was blind for an entire day. The Ron Arehucas probably contained a fair amount of methanol (wood spirit).

Three days ahead of our departure, the captain, Jean-Jacob, informed us of his change of plans. In order to expand upon the ship's coffers, he had entered into another business venture which entailed the transportation of two VW buses to Agadir, Morocco, for the sum of 500 dollars each. In advance, of course. After squeezing the buses into our cargo hold and unloading them in Agadir, we would embark on our Atlantic crossing. Our captain had thoroughly measured it all out and ensured everyone that the vehicles would fit just fine.

They did not fit just fine, but captain Jean-Jacob preferred not to accept this and, once more, disappeared with the money.

Madame, in despair, told us all to go to hell and locked herself in her cabin.

Me and my girlfriend decided to sign off this Jonah-haunted ship and return to the hostel. The Canadians and Madame's daughter joined us. One morning, *Carita* was gone, and no one knew where to, whereafter a carefree period started. We began roaming the quays in search of suitable passage to the West Indies. In this endeavour, we encountered some very odd individuals. Like Peter, an American living on a twenty-five-footer, literally entangled in seaweeds by a hidden corner of the harbor. He suffered from thalassophobia, fear of the ocean, a condition which was not too uncommon. It appears in the shape of an irrational panic and fear of the high seas. I have come upon many experienced boat owners who have been afflicted by it. It is unexplainable and sad. Peter had been struggling with it for two years, unable to cast off and cross the ocean.

And there was Dieter who lost his wife at sea, only three days out on the Atlantic, now situated onboard a German trawler. Ever since this tragic event took place, he had been successfully plundering wrecks with a crew of jail birds, one of the wrecks being a stranded oil tanker in the vicinity of Fuerteventura.

Another exceptional individual was Lennart, a Swedish businessman on the run from the tax authorities and hit men in Stockholm. The crew on his motor yacht consisted of, apart from members of his family, several lethal bodybuilders acting as his personal body guards. We were offered to join them to Venezuela, but politely declined.

At the innermost part of the harbor of Las Palmas, we spotted a huge three-mast-schooner, seemingly abandoned, or at least destined never to leave port again. We had just climbed onboard to have a look around when a middle-aged man appeared out of nowhere. He said something in Spanish, and I asked if he spoke English.

"Yes, of course," he answered, "I'm an educated man stuck with a task well beyond my capacity!"

Apparently, he used to work as a janitor, guarding the ship. His name was Tony, and he told us that the owners planned on sailing away to some distant shore... any year now. The large ship seemed to be in good shape, and I have always wondered what happened to her and Tony, the pleasant janitor and guardian of the ship.

Every now and then we came across modern sailing yachts in the process of leaving for the West Indies, but they were, sadly, in no need of additional crew. A French family on a forty-foot steel schooner with two small kids onboard almost signed us on. We pleaded and had our hopes up for a couple of days but had to give up when a relative of the wife showed up and stole our potential assignment.

Days went by, and we could not rid ourselves of a feeling of failure and hopelessness. The Canadians decided to take some time off and headed for the Gran Canaria mountains, while we desperately considered some alternative options. A small, well-built wooden sloop in the local boatyard caught our eye. It was for sale. Eagerly, we examined every inch of her. She seemed to be in fairly good condition – sails, rigging and a robust hull. But no engine. Ie pointed out:

"We've got the trade winds..."

What distracted us from that challenge was two merry Swedes on vacation, Larry, and Bobby. We bumped into them at a bar and immediately got acquainted with them, happily claiming the opportunity to speak Swedish again. Larry was a genuine sailing-ship-fanatic and, a couple of years earlier, he had crossed the Atlantic in a beautiful gaff-sloop, the *Nueva Flor*. Upon arriving in Barbados, he sold it to a wealthy American, returned to Sweden, and bought a Finnish sand cargo freighter (such as *Unicorn*, *Carita*, and *Marita*). Her name was *Mona of Borgå*.

Bobby was an out-and-out open-hearted scoundrel involved with shady, ongoing business ventures concerning various kinds of criminal networks. He carried incredible amounts of cash, spending it generously on all of us. Late one evening, after having treated us to champagne and caviar and Chivas Regal, he offered to take us to the West Indies in his own Catalina plane. Again, we politely declined, but promised to keep in touch. Just before they left, Larry asked if I would join him in Stockholm as his sailmaker's apprentice once I had returned home; thus, determining my future in ways I could only dream of at the time.

After a week of abundant, luxurious eating and drinking, we decided to join our Canadian friends in the mountains. It was time for a break in our search for marine transportation. We managed to contact them over the telephone, and they promised to come down, pick us up, and lead the way to a place best described as a forgotten Shangri-La. The bus carried us to the end of the road, leaving us to conquer the summit on foot. A three-hour exhausting hike followed, through ravines and over hill tops with slopes covered by lavender and rosemary. Along the narrow trail lined with almond trees, we passed small villages where time stood still, with villagers tending to traditional crafts and goat farming. As we were rapidly reaching the brink of collapse, cursing our heavy knapsacks, we heard George shout from ahead:

"Here it is!"

Right above an herb perfumed ascent along a red mountain ridge, a white clay house with glassless peepholes emerged, surrounded by ancient olive and almond trees, wild herbs, and unknown flower thickets. It seemed abandoned, but traces from random temporary visitors could be seen all over.

In the small back yard, a natural pool of cool spring water was carved into a hillside cave formation. The view was breath-taking, we could see the ocean glittering in the distance, in between the mountain slopes. The house did not seem to have an owner but served as a dwelling for anyone that happened to pass by. Supposedly, there was an unwritten law stating it was okay to occupy it for a while. It was a system that seemed to work very well.

The same rule applied to the numerous cave sites all over this mountain, for centuries used by sheep herders and outlaws, now home to hippies and globetrotters.

This was indeed a perfect place for rest and reflection, and well worth the trouble of getting here. We stayed for a week, resting our souls, hiking between the summits, visiting neighbouring caves, sharing exotic meals, and listening to Bob Dylan, The Band, and Hare Krishna, the sound of which bounced off of the mountain sides. Woodstock had emerged recently, and the universal brother- and sisterhood spirit was at its peak.

Whayne, who had returned after a trip to Las Palmas, excitedly told us about a boat in need of additional crew. Me and my girlfriend had all but given up hope of sailing across the great blue together. We had even considered asking our families for a loan to get tickets to Canada. This plan was enthusiastically endorsed by our friends, who argued that Ottawa was a far better place than Bridgetown, Barbados. But as it turned out, Whayne's information was correct. I went down to Las Palmas and could confirm that me and Ie were welcome aboard the catamaran *Chat Botté* bound for Quebec, but in need of crew for the crossing.

The owner Jean had bought the boat in England and was on his way home to Canada. On the same night that I returned to the mountain house, we had a farewell party and feasted on ham, bread, and wine. The following morning, we left our dear Canadian friends with little hope of ever seeing them again.

The Catamaran

We were heartily welcomed aboard by the skipper Jean. It was not a big boat, about 28 feet, but it was surprisingly roomy with its two hulls. The right hull had a well-equipped galley as well as my and Ie's cabin. The left hull had the skipper's cabin, a toilet, and a storage room. The hulls were connected by a small saloon with a table and a comfortable coach. In front of the mast, a net was suspended between the hulls, perfect for sunbathing.

A week of preparations followed; we were cleaning the bottoms, checking the sails, and did a general overhaul. Regrettably, we agreed to let Jean do the provisioning all by himself...

So, at last, on the morning of Mars 23rd in 1973, after having spent one and a half months in Gran Canaria, we were on our way, leaving the stinking harbor of Las Palmas behind. On the first day, slowly heading southwest in a moderate swell and light wind, we felt an indescribable relief as we watched the islands sink into the horizon.

The first night's watches were divided as follows: Jean 20:00-24:00, Me 24:00-04:00, and Ie 04:00-08:00.

On the morning of the second day at sea, the wind picked up from north-east, the seas were building up, and the air was filled with a fine, yellow dust. A scirocco storm from the Sahara Desert had caught up with us and kept intensifying, reaching 20m/s and gusting at 25-30m/s. The fine sand, almost like dust, found its way into every orifice – our eyes, our ears, and our mouth. The storm lasted for two days, creating huge waves that lifted our small boat up on top of them, only to speed back down again at 20 knots. It was like hurdling yourself off a ski slope with little to no rudder control. If one of the pontoons had cut down under water, we would have turned over and perished. It became a 48-hour struggle for our lives, without any sleep. Ie was hit with a severe case of seasickness and lost a lot of fluid. After ten hours of hell, she managed to sustain small amounts of orange juice.

With a fully reefed mainsail and a tiny storm jib, we flew across the furious sea, filled with anxiety, respect, and awe.

Finally, the storm ceased up, the sun came out, and a soft breeze swept in from the east. Gently, our minds got used to the thought of this being our home for an indefinite period of time.

That same afternoon we saw a boat ahead and, right before sundown, we caught up with her. Apparently, it was manned by two English gentlemen who had cast off a couple of days ahead of us. We exchanged positions, news, "good lucks", and parted in the fading light. These days, radio transmitters, GPS, and radar were scarce onboard small yachts, we had to rely on a chronometer sextant and a battery powered FM/AM radio for the BBC World News.

When the two Englishmen's boat had disappeared in the darkness, we knew that we were all alone and had to travel 2600 nautical miles to another continent before we could communicate with anyone else.

After a week of sailing on a south-westerly course, we luffed and steered 270 degrees due west with the trade winds, straight for Martinique in the French West Indies. If you steer west from the Canary Islands, you will risk ending up in the doldrums.

Finding our way across the Atlantic using only a sextant
(Photo the author)

Chat Botté had two tillers that enabled us to rig an ingenious self-steering solution by way of a rubber cord on one tiller and the jib sheet on the other, thus resulting in an excellent autopilot that only had to be adjusted from time to time. On the downside, it made the boat zig zag over long intervals, but that was clearly something we could live with. Quickly, we adjusted into our daily routines as we were carried westward by a friendly trade wind. Cooking, washing the dishes, checking the sails, rigging, and other miscellaneous chores of all sorts kept us busy.

Despite the steady wind, the heat kept on rising, forcing us to cool off with seawater every hour. Once every 24 hours, we had to charge the batteries using a horrible, tiny gasoline generator, but it had to be done in order to supply power to the lanterns. Setting up a sun tent, reading a good book, and regularly scanning the horizon was a favourite habit of mine. It does not take much imagination to envisage what Columbus and his crew felt sailing across this vast ocean, unknowing of whether or not they were headed towards the edge of the world...

Mending the sails on foredeck
(Photo: Ie Berger)

Once a day, just to ensure ourselves that the rest of the world was still there, we listened to the usual depressing events on BBC News, Vietnam, Watergate, the London Stock Exchange and April 8th, the death of Picasso.

Ten days out, the wind died down completely. The sea turned into an oily heaving eternity, releasing swarms of flying fish. Portuguese man O'war jellyfish slowly drifted past like small plastic bags. Two days and two nights we drifted with the westward current in an absolute calm. The heat started becoming almost unbearable. We spent most of those days hanging on to a rope in the water on the shady side of the boat.

The meals became important landmarks in our daily routines, even though they also, as time went by, became cumbersome. The first week, we could indulge ourselves in a variety of fresh oranges, tomatoes, onions, and salad, until the morning when the boat was filled with flies. The produce decayed quickly, and whatever we had not consumed up until that point had to be thrown overboard. Everything but the eggs. Smeared with Vaseline, they lasted the whole trip and tasted just fine. The rest of our provisions consisted of canned food with unknown contents, purchased by Jean. Soon we realised that our skipper had a passion for a variety of canned seafood such as sardines, mussels and, his favourite, squid submerged in its own ink. The few cans of corned beef and condensed milk were of little comfort. Jean argued that this type of food was the best you could eat, especially at sea. Being a loyal crew and realising that nothing could be done about the ship's supplies, we tried our best to refine this disgusting raw material into eatable dishes. What ultimately improved the situation was some dried pea soup and rice porridge that my mother forced me to bring along as "emergency" food, which became culinary highlights in between the tinned squid.

Our fresh water was kept in rubber tanks inside the stern compartments of the hulls. 11 days out, it was undrinkable, having the taste and smell of burnt rubber. Foreseeing this problem, we rationed the 24 bottles of mineral water.

A whale sighting!
(Photo: the author)

Reflecting on the reason for making a voyage like this sometimes overwhelmed us. The loneliness and, above all, the feeling of insignificance brought on by travelling in a fragile man-made shell across a vast ocean, made us aware of our vulnerability. On the ocean's terms, we sailed over depths that could engulf us without a trace. The outcome was dependent our own knowledge and technology, and no mercy could be expected if we made misjudgements or showed a lack of humility.

Our keels engraved an impermanent, rapidly disappearing trace on the element that covers three fourths of the earth's surface and is, in fact, the place of our own origin. After 14 days in a circle of unbroken horizon, this was quite a frequently visited subject.

We measured the suns altitude every day and added another couple of millimetres' worth of pencil line onto the chart. Halfway across, the moments with the sextant became almost sacred and, although we knew we still had a long way to travel, we continued to keep a lookout for land.

Late in the afternoon on the second day of dead calm, we spotted a cargo ship by the horizon. They altered their course and headed straight towards us. They manned the railings, waved, and sounded their horn. We gave a "thumbs up", letting them know that all was well with us, and they resumed their course, heading north-west.

We had been out at sea for 15 days when we first saw them: whales of a, for us, unknown kind, playing around us and underneath us. After suddenly disappearing for a few minutes, they emerged right beside the boat, blowing cascades of water into the air. They were the same length as our boat, if not longer, and could easily have flipped us over, dispatching us into oblivion. Playful and carefree, they stayed with us until nightfall, which is when they took off towards the setting sun.

The trade wind blew evenly from the east or north-east between 4 and 10 m/s. We travelled at an average of 130-200 nautical miles per day. The days were filled with routines, and we adapted to our new limited environment; a square shaped catamaran, a small space restricted by the railing supports. In this micro world, we evolved into a well-functioning unit, but we did not talk much anymore. Words had been replaced by gestures. The sea was endless, but gave us the best of days, the sun rising in the east as we woke and setting beyond our bow. It demonstrated a display of colours that left us breathless.

Washing the dishes
(Photo: Ie Berger)

On my watch at night, I often disconnected the self-steering just to have something to occupy myself with. Millions of stars punctured the violet night, and, behind the pendulating mast, I kept our course directed towards the constellation of Libra. Flying fish revealed themselves with phosphorus streaks, and sometimes I could sense the sounds and movements of larger creatures in the depths. A cup of strong coffee diluted with sweet, condensed milk lasted me an hour and tasted like heaven in combination with the Capstan tobacco in my pipe.

Just before dawn, I felt like I was a part of everything, included in a universal context – a bewildering but wonderful sensation. When eight bells approached and my eyelids grew heavy, I started yearning for my preheated bunk.

The West Indies

It had been 20 days at sea, and we were getting closer to land. Our navigation was not 100% accurate, which is why keeping a sharp lookout was necessary. Ie and I began spending the nights together, listening to the sound of the surf.

On April 14th, we huddled in the cockpit, making good speed in the north-easterly trade wind. The skipper was always heavily asleep with his porthole open, snoring loudly. An exceptional number of flying fish kept landing on deck, of which one landed in my lap. We held on to a few of them for breakfast: crispy fried flyfish, fried eggs, and a ratatouille made from canned tomatoes was a well-needed break from the otherwise prevailing culinary disaster. With weary eyes, we scanned the horizon for any sign of land and, around 03:00 a.m., we both saw it. Something swept the sky, or was it an illusion? We were not supposed to make landfall until mid-day but kept our eyes scouting due west. And there it was again! A recurring cone of light! I rushed down to get the chart and wake Jean. Checking the chart confirmed that the light was emanating from the lighthouse Rocque de Diamond on the easterly point of Martinique. We praised the skipper for his navigational skills and opened a bottle of Canary champagne. In silence, we regarded the welcoming light cone sweeping across the Caribbean night sky.

At first daylight, we sighted the silhouette of Martinique's volcanic mountain range, and by noon we reached Roque de Diamond on the rugged east coast of the island. Since we had been up all night, our weariness made us less alert and unaware of the approaching squall. A black, malicious cloud came rushing towards us. These local storms could appear in a matter of minutes and disappear just as quickly. They could easily de-mast a ship or boat in seconds, shredding all sails and washing the crew overboard. Jean and I panicked and struggled with lowering the mainsail, but when only about 50 meters remained before we were caught by raging wind and rain, the storm changed course and swept north, as if we were too small a vessel to demolish. Shocked and boosted with adrenaline, we set sail again, rounded Roque de Diamond, and sailed along the coast to Fort de France, the capital of Martinique.

Roque de Diamond, Martinique.
(Photo: the author)

Fort de France is situated at the end of a bay, leeward and well sheltered from the trade winds. Along the seashore, a row of white, beautiful colonial houses and palm trees lined the beach. By the southern end of the bay, the city streets turned into a white and inviting beach.

Just outside the marina, we anchored and hoisted the yellow quarantine flag. Half an hour later, the customs official appeared in his dinghy. In accordance with old traditions, he was bribed with whiskey and cigarettes, whereafter he stamped our passports and went back ashore. A few meters out, he dutifully turned around and shouted:

"You are all well I presume...no illnesses onboard?"

While awaiting customs, we washed ourselves in the remaining, disgusting, smelly fresh water, put on clean clothes, and inflated our rubber dinghy. And now, having been cleared by customs, we went ashore.

23 days at sea can have strange consequences on a person's sense of balance. Resembling three drunken, tanned, sea-wretched phantoms, we wobbled through the streets and alleys. Jean faltered away on his own while Ie and I were desperately determined to find a special place. And we did not have to look very far. Under a gigantic tin roof supported by ornamented cast iron pillars, a marketplace spread out in front of us. Tropical fruits, vegetables, and spices stored in huge piles were being guarded by fat ladies in colourful dresses. We stopped for a while, in awe of the pyramids of pineapples, mangoes, limes, bananas, lemons, and coconuts as well as the large baskets of cinnamon, cloves, and different kinds of pepper. There were also small market stands serving freshly pressed sugar cane juice with ice and lime.

Our longing for fresh fruit had turned into a desperate craving. At sea, we chewed on vitamin C tablets to nourish our yearning. Now, our bodies were demanding the real thing. In the market centre, a small square was spared to make room for chairs that tired shoppers could rest in, sipping on their coffee or tea. A small truck reversed and situated itself right beside the coffee counter, unloading a couple cubic meters of pineapples. The golden fruits were two to three times larger than the ones we had seen before, and we got two of them for 10 francs. Without a word, we tore one apart and buried our faces in it. It was heavenly and indescribable, something which just has to be experienced.

When we had calmed down, dripping of pineapple juice, fully satiated, we noticed that the commerce and coffee drinking around us had come to a halt. Instead, the good citizens of Fort de France had silently witnessed a display of Nordic berserk, performed on pineapples.

Shamefully, we retreated into the sunshine and sat down on a bench outside the PTT, a telegraph's office. We realised that we somehow had to let our parents know where we were, especially since we never told them that we actually found a way of passage across the Atlantic. They had not heard a word from us in over three weeks. Telegrams were ridiculously expensive, so we limited ourselves to three words:

Martinique
I and B

Monsieur Raoul

For a week, everything was perfect. We were mostly swimming, diving, drinking sugar cane juice, and basically living off mangos. But, as the week came to an end, we had to make a decision. We were more than welcome to stay on the *Chat Botté* and sail with Jean all the way to Canada, but a gentleman on a big French ketch gave us an offer we could not refuse. Without having seen his boat we accepted and, the day after, we bid a somewhat sad farewell to Jean and signed on to the *S/Y Amphora*. Later that same day, we saw Jean heave anchor and set course for his distant homeland, the flag of Quebec proudly fluttering from the back stay. We never heard from him again, but we found out from elsewhere that he finally made it to his homeport.

The owner of *Amphora*, Monsieur Raoul D, was in desperate need of a crew for his recently purchased yacht. We were offered generous compensation if we could also help him get the ship in order.

S/Y Amphora was in a terrible state. Supposedly, she was the sister of a yacht owned by Hermann Göring, built in Holland in the '30s. Her steel hull had beautiful lines. 14 meters in overall length, ketch rigged with a mizzen, mainsail, jib, and an outer jib. She also had a roomy salon with exquisitely carved ornaments and mahogany panelling, three big cabins and a well-equipped galley and head. Previously, she had been an extravagant yacht, proudly travelling the seas. Now, she was a study in rust and decay. The ancient, rust-free rigging was breaking apart in several places. The glass in the skylight, together with the glass in almost every porthole, was shattered. All the woodwork was cracked or rotten and had not seen new varnish since the Korean war. I almost dare not speak of the sails, made from synthetic fibre and long past their best-before date. The engine room was a nightmare, harbouring equipment from the days of World War II. The gasoline powered engine itself was covered in rust, oil, and old rags. All of the electrical wiring was chafed and likely to produce random sparks at any moment.

Raoul was a young nobleman, an aristocrat, born in the wrong century. Without a doubt, he would have fit in on the bridge of a frigate during the Napoleon Wars. His point of view was that "the flaws of *Amphora* were minor problems which preferably shouldn't even be discussed, just be taken care of".

With polite and kind nonchalance, he dismissed my carefully submitted proposition that the ship had to have a complete and thorough make-over to safely transport any paying charter passenger, which was his ambition. With divine patience, he explained to us that his future customers were to exclusively be recruited from the French colonial upper class.

We hopelessly got to work with whatever means we had at hand. All the woodwork that was not rotten had to be scraped down and revarnished. Brass fittings came to life after years of negligence. After a trying rust removal (where we had to be careful not to cause any more cavities), we managed to restore a relatively decent finish on the hull. Turning the engine room into a safe place to run the engine seemed to be an impossible task, but after a week of cleaning and replacing all the wiring, the result was astonishing. The only troublesome task concerning the engine itself was the changing of all the pipes and reassuring that all the gasoline leaks were fixed. And Raoul was pleased. With dramatic gestures and satisfied growling, he spent his days inspecting our progress and pointing out new chores with his bamboo stick. To be fair, he was truly an excellent employer who never interfered and, without any shame, admitted that he knew nothing about how to maintain a boat. And he was a fantastic cook, providing meals from the French-Creole cuisine. And, most importantly, he paid us the agreed salary every Friday, on time. All in all, he kept us happy and boosted our motivation to succeed in doing the impossible. Our working days passed at a laid-back, West Indies pace, well-adjusted to the prevailing climate. When the noon temperature rose to about 40°C, we just had to get out of the sun and cool off by whatever means possible, i.e., slide into the water on the shady side of the boat.

The fact that the main local beverage (sugar cane juice with lime, ice, and a few drops of 1925 dark rum) was growing on us, did nothing to improve our productivity. The Jamaican reggae station contributed to a swift adjustment to local customs. *Amphora* was anchored just above an old wreck, fully visible at a mere three meters below the surface. As we were snorkelling and hovering nearby, we got to witness hundreds of different fish in every imaginable colour.

Often, we let ourselves drift onto the beach, resting under shadowy palm trees and overindulging on fresh mango, sold by proud ladies carrying baskets on top of their heads. When a velvet dusk fell over Fort de France, we cleaned up and put on the best clothes we had to enjoy another surprise culinary dinner onboard. Some examples of which included Cajun spiced lobster tails with pineapples au gratin or a fresh salad with coconut dressing and garlic bread, all accompanied by a young rosé wine or an ice-cold beer. The evening meals always ended with a glass of dark, mellow Martinique rum, aged for 40 years with a moderate sweetness and underlying tones of roasted spices.

The salon, with its dark brown mahogany and eucalyptus panelling and old-fashioned velvet cushions, created an atmosphere of reflection and inspired us to share stories from all around the world. A solid brass lamp swayed slowly, casting shadows on the bulkheads, permitting us all to forget the ship's terrible condition for a moment and think of times long past.

Raoul, always clad in a spotless tropical suit, told us of his time in the Foreign Legion and made-up tales of sailing in Scandinavian waters. A cool evening breeze swept through the skylight and carried scents of coconut fires from the small villages further down the bay. Around 09:00 p.m., we used to row into the city to stroll around and explore the various establishments of this picturesque capital.

After two weeks, Raoul informed us that he had arranged for us to get *Amphora* out of the water in Barbados for a hull inspection, scraping and painting. With emphasis, he told us about the difficulties in establishing an agreement with those "English-speaking morons". But, after many phone calls and letters, he finally reached a valid agreement. Four days later, we heaved anchor and left for Bridgetown Barbados. *Amphoras* hull was covered with a very thick layer of marine life forms under the waterline, some of which we could scrape off using the dinghy. Despite our efforts, with all sails up and the motor running, we only made three knots during our three-day passage, rather than the one-day passage we had anticipated.

To make things worse, we were all affected by severe diarrhoea, caused by the heaving, stirring old water tanks releasing malignant microorganisms. I will refrain from revealing what I found in those water tanks when I cleaned them, later on...

Taking turns at the helm in intervals of about five minutes, we finally made it to the British Colony of Barbados, anchoring outside the old Imperial Yacht Club.

Dehydrated and worn out from the passage, we slept a whole day. I always carry charcoal tablets with me wherever I go, which turned out to be a blessing. Even Raoul reluctantly swallowed a couple, and, in the evening, we felt strong enough for a visit ashore.

The once upon a time proud and well managed yacht club, an important part of the British colonial rule, was now in a state of disrepair. The remaining members, all upper-class gentlemen in their 70s or over, spent their days reading newspapers while drinking tea and Port served by elderly native servants. The buildings and tennis courts were falling apart, slowly being reclaimed by nature. The "private" beach was occupied by children of all ages, and Atlantic swells were wearing down the formerly luxurious private harbor where brass shining yachts and steam sloops used to moor.

But the club's showers were in order, displaying beautiful sculptures of Venus and Poseidon with mosaic floors, and we could indulge ourselves in a long, recuperating wash.

The morning after, Raoul headed off to let the boatyard know we had arrived and were ready to be hauled out of the water. A few hours later he returned, steaming with rage. The yard owner had acted surprised and was completely baffled, informing Raoul that there was not a chance in the world for *Amphora* to get on the slip. At least not for a couple of weeks…

Raoul desperately tried to refer to their telephone call a week ago:

"You told me 'Yes, possible to get up this week!'"

The yard owner had answered, laconically:

"No man, I said 'Not possible this week, too much work now.' Way too much to do man. You got me wrong man, sorry…" Whereupon he shrugged his shoulders and returned to an ongoing game of whist in his office.

While attempting to restrain his frustration, Raoul observed that the boatyard was empty with nothing going on, like an abandoned railway yard.

"I'll try again tomorrow," he growled and went into his cabin.

In an attempt to appease him, we decided to make dinner, but our Scandinavian cooking skills only seemed to make things worse. We just had to let things settle and await further orders.

Raoul was gone the rest of the following day, so we spent hours snorkelling along the beach in the company of a shoal of barracudas.

At nightfall, he returned carrying bags of groceries, mostly delicatessen of all sorts. We noticed he was not completely unaffected but decided not to ask any questions.

"Well, my friends, as you might be able to guess there will be no boatyard for us on this island," he closed his eyes for a second, exhaled, and continued, "but I can ensure you one thing – we are going to have a fantastic supper, drink lots of wine, and in the morning, we will return to Martinique! And, besides, there has to be more than one boatyard in this part of the world… I'll be happy to sail away from these English-speaking nincompoops…!"

He did not reveal what had happened in the boatyard, but we noticed that his suit had black marks on the back and that one sleeve was torn.

Sailing back to Martinique was equally as frustrating as sailing from it. We were making two to three knots in the small trade wind gale, but we had brought a lot of mineral water this time.

It was the end of May and the constant heat started to take its toll on these two northerners. The yearning for a cool summer morning with dewy grass became almost overwhelming. At this time, we had made enough money to pay for a flight home, and we booked tickets on Icelandair on a set date.

Raoul was not happy. In fact, he became furious, accusing us of treason and sabotage since there was so much more to be done on *Amphora*. But he calmed down and apologised, yet bitterly regretted having to be left alone in the middle of this great project. We had long since given up on trying to convince him that this ship could never serve as a charter vessel, but tried to encourage him by reassuringly saying that there would be other able craftsmen to employ. For sure. Especially if he kept serving up extraordinary dinners. Susceptible to all forms of praise, he regained his good mood and told us that we had been invited to join him for dinner at some friend's place in the mountains.

"It will be my farewell dinner for you, my Swedish friends, and in addition you will be able to enjoy more of the French cuisine!"

The evening before our departure, we were picked up by a young Frenchman and his fiancée in a Renault 4, which is a very small car. I had to sit in the luggage compartment, something that turned out to be an endurance test I had never experienced before and would never forget. We were headed towards a small cocoa farm close to the volcano of Mount Pelée. The road was narrow with no space for any approaching vehicles, on one side the rocky mountainside, on the other a steep ravine. The young man drove at a death-defying speed, making the wheels clutch to the edge of the road.

Upon arrival, we were alive but pale, sweaty, and secretly agreeing to walk back to Fort de France. We were well received by our hosts and offered enormous rum drinks. Since English was not spoken in this family, I struggled to maintain a decent conversation while translating to Ie. Eventually, the moment arrived which Raoul had spoken of so enthusiastically. Our hostess invited us to be seated at the extravagantly laid table – it had crystal glasses, gold ornamented dishes, and antique chandeliers. Above us, an old Bleriot propeller slowly rotated, creating a cool breath of air. She solemnly announced the beginning of what was meant to be a culinary experience, something out of the ordinary. Two native servants appeared, carrying trays loaded with different glass cups containing square pieces of something unknown to us. We were hit with a stale, cadaverous scent, and served substantial portions of "entrailles" (cow's stomach pickled in salt and cured in a warm place).

The taste cannot be described in words, but it is worth a try: imagine bloated pieces of sole leather steaming with an odour of dirty socks and a damp towel, having been forgotten behind the washing machine, floating in a slimy liquid which smells of old flower water.

Everybody praised the hostess for her remarkable kitchen skills.

With the help of way too much wine, we finished everything on our plate and politely declined a refill, in an attempt to avoid hurting anyone's feelings or appearing ungrateful. For dessert, we were served a tasteless jelly and cheese, which made me realise that Camembert, Brie and Livarot does not thrive in the tropics.

At midnight, we bid them farewell, ensuring our hosts that we would never forget this evening. We insisted on walking back to town but were promptly dismissed by the son of the house. Luckily, his parents realised he was in no state to drive and suggested that his fiancée give us a ride. In pitch black darkness and at the speed of a turtle, we safely arrived at the harbor. We fell asleep with rumbling stomachs, having set an alarm for 07:00 a.m.

A small, pink coloured, twin-engine plane with oil stripes along the fuselage carried us back to Barbados. Beneath us, the blue waters of the Caribbean instilled a sense of melancholy. Was this a mistake, leaving now instead of exploring more of these beautiful islands in the trade winds? Chances were that we would never return. But in our hearts, we knew nothing could keep us from heading back to the cool Nordic summer.

Icelandic Air's crowded DC 8 bumped away on the neglected Georgetown runway, barely making it over the palm trees, climbed above the clouds, and set course for Luxembourg.

Epilogue

Many years later, while writing this book, I came across an article in a Swedish newspaper. It was about a man from Bolivia, now living in southern Sweden, testifying that he knew the truth about the assassination of Che Guevara. In the article, he stated that a certain Monsieur Raoul D had taken an active part in the betrayal of the communist leader, all fiercely denied by French officials and spokesmen. It was soon forgotten, and the Bolivian man passed away shortly after.

I did some research and could confirm that this was the same Raoul D we had worked for in Martinique. After googling him, I learned that he had been imprisoned in Bolivia but released with the help of Jean Paul Sartre, De Gaulle, and the Pope Paulus VI. For some reason, Raoul D. had to reside in Martinique for a couple of years.

D. returned to France, became involved in politics, and founded a new scientific discipline combining the study of culture with the study of technology.

Curious about whatever happened to him and his boat, I tried to reach out via his office in Paris. One day, I got him on the phone, but he was not really interested in talking to me and asked me to write him a letter, which I did, but he never replied.

My letter to Mr. Raoul D

Järvsö, Sweden November 12, 2007

Dear Mr. D!

First of all, I apologise for calling you last Monday morning! I understand that you are a busy man and that my phone call may have come at an inconvenient time. My poor French probably did not improve upon things either. So, sorry about that!

My reason for contacting you is as follows:

In 2001, I wrote a book about my travels at sea (Tales from the Sea) in which I described me and my fiancé's journey in 1973 from Gran Canaria to Martinique in the catamaran "Chat Botté", owned by a Mr. Jean Allard of Quebec.

In this story, there is a tale of a French gentleman by the name of Raoul D, who cooked the most fantastic meals while me and my fiancé (Ie) tried to restore the old steel ketch that he wanted to use for charter in the French West Indies. Among other things, we sailed to Barbados to get to a shipyard, but failed, and had to return to Fort de France. Mr. D had some friends up in the mountains who we paid a visit to. They also treated us to "tripe", which left a somewhat dubious impression on my culinary memory...

The suicidal trip to these friends in a small Renault 4 (where I was placed in the trunk) also left a vivid imprint.

It was not until recently, when I noticed the name Raoul D, (philosopher, intellectual, writer etc.) on the internet that I came to wonder if this could be the same man!

I remember him telling us that he had spent a lot of time in South America and he, with some moderation, shared his story with us.

We had a fantastic time in Martinique, and I remember Mr. D as a very pleasant man whom we shared many memorable moments with. During the Caribbean nights, we would sit in the lounge onboard, drinking marvellous old Martinique rum, telling stories, and discussing existential matters.

In my book, it also turned into a good story, <u>but I would</u>
<u>really like to know what happened to the boat!</u>

So, voilà, my reason for calling you! <u>To find out if it</u>
<u>was you!?</u>

As for myself, I am amid a literary career. And, just
recently, I have been given the honourable task (by Mr.
Sture Allén of the Swedish Academy) to write a book
about one of Sweden's most beloved poets Evert Taube
(1890-1976) who, by the way, lived in Antibes for a
long time. He is also known for having made excellent
translations of French medieval poems. My publisher is
Norstedts in Stockholm, and I will be publishing three
books over the course of the next year.

If you are the same Raoul D that I met in Martinique
some 35 years ago, and if you can find the time, please
write me a couple of lines!

With all respect,
Yours faithfully!

Birger Sjöberg

NB: Out of discretion the name Raoul D is made up.

ANNA OF RISÖR

*"What are dreams but
Expectations seen through.
a veil of ignorance..."*

Length: 11 meters. Beam: ca 4 meters. Built in 1917 in Risör, Norway by shipwright Knutsen. Sloop rigged in the beginning and eventually equipped with a 15 Hp Brunvold semi diesel. Originally in service as a rescue boat on the Norwegian west coast. Most likely used for coastal fishing later on.

The noble art of buying a boat.

I turned 21 and started dreaming of getting a ship of my own. As I had now become of age, some inheritance was passed down from my late grandmother which made this possible, and so I started scanning the market for something beautiful and reliable. Many attempts were made, mostly by my mother, to talk me in to saving the money for future investments such as studies, a house, or a car, but all her efforts were futile. Nothing was to stand in the way of my dream. I really do not recall how I got in touch with the owner of a Norwegian-built former rescue boat, but probably through an ad in the newspaper. I was informed that the boat was on land, right by the stream Stångån in Linköping.

A beautiful spring day in 1974, I went to inspect her with a friend and fell in love immediately. She was a beauty with a sturdy, buoyant hull and slender lines resembling a Colin Archer design. No rot or soft spots, however the deck could use some new planking. The engine room was well equipped with new fuel tanks and batteries, the main engine being a six-cylinder Volvo diesel of approximately 100 hp. In combination with the huge two-blade propeller, there undoubtedly was enough power.

There were no cabins or other interior carpentry, except for a bulkhead to the engine room, which did not bother me in the least since I wanted to custom-make the inside layout.

On the downside, the rigging was in poor shape. A rusty tabernacle and three shrouds supported a short steel mast, only capable of carrying a small mainsail and a jib. I visualised her gaff rigged with two masts and a long bow sprit. It was the ideal hull, sharp lines, and a great underwater shape. The deal included a substantial load of oak planks, ropes, and various tools. He wanted 17,000 Swedish crowns, which was a true bargain. I was left with 3,000 – enough money to pay for the trip home and to get more materials.

After a swift handshake, the deal was made. It was the end of May, and spring was just about to turn into summer. Exhilarated, we returned home to pick up more equipment and enrol one more crew member. But there was not much time, because a bridge across the river was under construction and we could risk being trapped with the frogs and perches. Being the third mate, I asked my friend and colleague from Denmark, George, to join us. We had worked together as sailmakers in Denmark, and he was an excellent craftsman with only one vital flaw – he had never sailed before. In fact, he had never been out at sea at all, unless you count a ferry-ride between our two countries. So, this was his opportunity to correct that.

Farewell to Linköping

With my small car loaded way beyond its capacity, we returned to *Anna* a week later. My brother Lars volunteered to drive the car back home. Meanwhile, the former owner, a nice middle-aged man, had applied antifouling on the boat, lifted her into the water, and left everything in ship-shape. And there she was, gently resting in her right element, beautiful beyond my wildest dreams.

The lumber-cargo was secured well, creating a temporary floor in the cargo room where all the equipment was stored. Up on deck, we arranged for a simple but functional galley, and sturdy fenders were placed along the railings for the first part of the voyage through the Göta Canal and its many locks. Until the very last minute, I hesitated about the route we would take home. It would be safer to travel the canal all the way to Gothenburg, but it would also be a lot more expensive. Our meagre funds pushed me to make a fatal decision – to go via the Baltic Sea to Öresund, Kattegat and, finally, Skagerrak. And I felt confident about it. Anna was built for the high seas, no worries…

June 3rd,1974, we cast off and started heading east towards the Baltic Sea, barely making it underneath the new bridge construction site. I immediately felt that the boat was over-powered and decided to never exceed a 50% throttle, since her stern would just dig down and not make better speed than eight knots anyway.

It was a beautiful early summer, with leafy, green canal banks and birds, having returned from their migration, nesting in every tree and bush. At a moderate pace, we made good headway, enjoying every minute of our trip. Luncheon was served on deck, boiled eggs along with pickled and freshly smoked herring. With us being a crew of five, passing the locks went smoothly and, before nightfall, we entered the Baltic Sea and moored in Söderköping. Tired but in high spirits, we all went to sleep below deck. Around 3:00 a.m., heavy rain turned the cargo hold into a shower, allowing jets of water to find its way into our sleeping bags and blankets. Shivering underneath a huge tarpaulin, the crew endured until dawn, when my brother and his fiancé hurried back to Stockholm.

The three of us – Olaf, Georg, and I – cast off and set course for the town of Västervik, travelling through the breathtakingly beautiful archipelago of St. Anna and Gryt. This particular stretch of the Swedish east coast is known for its lush and idyllic waterways. Small, tree covered islands with small farms and pastures make you feel like you are travelling back in time, witness to an echo from days and people long gone.

Late that night, we reached Västervik and enjoyed a shower, phoned home, and went to sleep underneath the tarpaulin.

June 5th brought a change of weather, clouds and mist drifted in from north-west with increasing wind. We had breakfast on deck, feasting on freshly baked buns from the bakery across the street. After having secured the rig and our two sails, we plotted our next stretch, down south to Kråkelund. We also planned on taking a detour to the island Öland and the small village Byxelkrok. Heading south by south-east, we made good headway and spotted Öland after only a few hours. An elderly gentleman offered us smoked flatfish, which we enjoyed along with some Swedish rye bread and beer. Byxelkrok has a well-sheltered harbor but, in the middle of the night, I awoke from the sound of waves breaking over the pier. I went up on deck to check on the lines and enjoy the wind along with the early summer night scenery. The wind had shifted to south-west and was steadily increasing. I felt happy. I was heading home with a ship of my own and, given some time, I would soon be conquering the seas and building the future of my dreams. In youthful exuberance, I visualised my coming adventures, unaware of what destiny had in store.

The shipwreck

June 6th, 1974, the Swedish National Day. The wind had shifted south, increased to 12 metres per second, and white, foamy waves were rushing north through the Kalmar Strait. The weather report promised a decrease in wind later on during the day, and we decided to carry on after breakfast. *Anna* moved nicely in the heavy seas, breaking the waves with her buoyant bow, causing next to no spray at all. The current was flowing north, and at half speed, we set course for the small town Borgholm. The Kalmar Strait grew more and more narrow, and the waves became shorter and steeper. I reduced the speed to one quarter.

One of Olaf's tasks was to check the engine every half hour and Georg kept an eye on the bilge pumping every now and then. At 11:30 that morning, Olaf went down to the engine room for the third time. Seconds later, he was back on deck.

"We've got a leak!"

With a rush of adrenalin, I threw myself down the hatch, only to find the seawater raising above the propeller shaft. I immediately turned the throttle to idle and put the gear in neutral.

"Try to keep her upwind!" I shouted to Georg at the helm. With my body halfway under water, I examined the area closest to the stern where the propeller shaft met the stern timber. I immediately felt it, a huge hole on the port side. Parts of the planking had opened, which caused the sea to begin rushing in.

A mixture of panic, powerlessness, and fear came over me for a few seconds, as if my own blood was rushing out at the same pace that the water was rushing in. I shouted, at the top of my lungs:

"Georg! Pump the bilge!"

Hastily, we all agreed on the need for immediate assistance, and I went to get the emergency flares from inside the chest on foredeck. Olaf scanned the horizon and suddenly caught sight of a coast guard cruiser far away, nearby the mainland, on starboard bow. I ripped open the flare container, aimed it in front of the coast guards, and fired it. The rocket arose at a perfect arc, just in front of them, but remained unseen. The second flare did not reach far enough and was not seen either.

Anna was now swaying heavily in the rough seas at a surreal slow-motion pace. Every other wave was now crashing down on deck as we were furiously pumping, only managing to slightly delay the rising of the water. In vain, we tried to stop the leak from the inside, but the water pressure was too high and, submerged in the oily water, all I could establish was that the planking had opened up even more.

It had only been minutes since we discovered the leak, and now we had started realising that our lives were at stake. The short periods under water made my limbs numb, and I knew we would not last long in the freezing spring seas. With the engine in gear once more, I put it into full throttle, heading straight for Borgholm while we searched for any signs of other ships. But, in June, these waterways are just about deserted, as the main shipping lines pass by on the other side of Öland.

Suddenly, with my binoculars directed towards the horizon, I could discern the contour of a small ship heading south, growing bigger by the minute, and decided to set course straight towards it. Since we had no radio transmitter, we knew this was our only chance. Georg and I took turns pumping and Olaf held on to the forestay signalling, containing the remaining hand flares. The water had now filled up halfway to the air intake of the roaring engine. *Anna* plunged through the sea like a half-submerged tank, rushing towards our salvation. The hull shivered violently, as if she were struggling with her own downfall. The wind eased up a bit, the waves seemed to decrease in height, and the visibility became better. Our downwind direction alleviated the pressure on the leak, and, for a while, we could keep up with the pump. A warming sun appeared in between the chasing clouds as we were fighting for our lives.

Olaf lit the hand flares one by one and was surrounded by a thick magnesium smoke resembling a ghostly sea creature on a temporary visit in the world of the living. The cargo ship was still far away, and I wondered if they would notice us or pass us by, leaving the crew of *Anna* to perish in the freezing waters of the Kalmar Strait. I continuously tracked the cargo ship with my binoculars, hoping that she will change her course with every passing minute. Olaf had run out of flares, so I grabbed the flagpole with the oversized Swedish flag attached to it and showed him how to wave it back and forth as a distress signal. When I turned around, Georg had passed out on deck from exhaustion and, as I tried to get him back on his feet, he vomited. However, throwing up seemed to revive him and, without a word, he continued to pump. I returned my focus to the distant, possible rescue, but there was still no change in bearing. She seemed to keep a straight southerly course, which means she was set to pass several miles west of us. Then, unexpectedly, I spotted a burst of black smoke and her silhouette changed! They had spotted us and were headed our way at full speed. I vaguely heard her sound the ship's horn; repeatedly blaring four short signals, letting us know she was coming to assist. The relief is hard to describe, knowing we were going to be rescued, saved from an early death. As the small cargo ship approached, I could read her name on the bow: *Susanne of Stockholm*. With a foaming surge, she rushed towards us and was eventually alongside *Anna*, close enough for us to communicate. At this moment, I noticed that I was completely soaked and shaking from the icy water, whereas my face and hair were smeared with oil and my heart furiously beating.

Susanne was a very small cargo ship. She was old, weathered, rusty, and I could hear the comforting sound of her engine; 7-cylindre motor: NV Machinefabriek Bolne. *Susanne's* captain leaned out of the Wheel house and shouted:

"How long can you hold out for?"

I replied:

"Maybe fifteen minutes… maybe half an hour…!" He nodded and said something to his radio operator.

"We have notified the coast guards… They are not far away and should be here shortly! We don't have any portable pumps, but I can have someone from my crew come over to you if you want!"

"Well, I think we can stay afloat if we just keep on pumping, but thanks anyway! And thanks a million for coming to our assistance!"

"Okay, you're welcome! I'll stay with you until I know you're all right!"

Trying to keep her afloat
(Photo: Georg Jensen)

I relieved George at the pump, he was completely exhausted and just slumped down on deck. Olaf began gathering all our belongings – sleeping bags, tools, two guitars, and three knapsacks. As the minutes went by, we slowly drifted away from *Susanne,* and I steered upwind to get closer. But, after only a few yards, the water reached the air intake of the motor, and it went forever silent. Just in case, the crew on *Susanna* readied a lifeboat, but by now the coast guards had arrived and stopped alongside *Anna.*

I shouted:

"Can you get a little bit closer so that we have a chance to save our belongings?"

Being towed
(Photo: The Swedish coastguards)

To my surprise, he answered:

"We must tow you out of the shipping line first!" His words were followed by the throwing of a heavy towing line. I wondered what difference it would make if we sank here, at the depth of one hundred meters, or somewhere else, since anyone could see that *Anna* only had a few minutes of keeping afloat left. Nevertheless, I realised it was no time for arguing and secured the line around the mast, whereafter ten minutes of towing began. *Anna* had sunk deep into the water now, but our cargo of planks most likely dragged out the final showdown. George kept on pumping, despite being on the brink of collapse, with blood coming out of his nose. Olaf was soaked in seawater and oil from his attempts to stop the leak, his clothes all torn. I passed out life jackets and told my crew to prepare themselves to abandon ship. The coast guards now found it suitable to stop towing us and came to a full stop some 20 meters away. In vain, I pleaded to them to come a little bit closer, but they shook their heads and manned the railing to watch the end of it all and take pictures...

June 6, icy waters
(Photo: The Swedish coastguards)

Many things of considerable value could have been saved: two compasses, all the hand tools (including my collection of adzes), a radio direction finder, a complete Walkers Log, charts, a Primus burner, two brand new fire extinguishers, and much more. When we only had minutes left before sinking, I ordered my crew to jump overboard and swim over to the coast guard. When I could see that they were safe, I climbed atop *Anna's* bow and, when I could feel it raising, I threw myself in the cold Baltic Sea and swam towards my own salvation. For a moment, Anna seemed to hesitate but, soon after, she disappeared beneath the surface. A small swirl, and she was gone.

Paralysed by emotions and *coldness, I crawled aboard the coast guard's boat. A June sun broke through the clouds and made her deck steam. On the now calm sea, our floatable belongings slowly scattered: two trunks, two guitars, and three sleeping bags, the rest was gone. Strangely enough, the coast guard captain now offered to try to salvage what could be saved. Everything except for two blankets was pulled onboard.

The lost dream
(Photo: The Swedish coastguards)

In the neatly kept engine room, we restored our body temperatures while barely saying a word, contemplating our gloomy faith. It was no time for words, and, in silent understanding, we agreed on the fact that we will need time to digest, time to mourn, and time to appreciate the fact that we survived. Upon arrival at the port of Borgholm, I was called to the commander to, with numb hands, fill out a report. A pile of our wet belongings rested on the pier, and, in silence, we watched the coast guards cast off. I can still hear the merry words of farewell from the captain:

"Well boys, sad story this… But I'm sure there will be another ship waiting for you somewhere! *And… I don't think it would have helped to use the two 300 litres per minute pumps that we had onboard…!*

You will just have to be grateful to be alive… And, by the way Mr. Sjoberg, you must prepare to face some dire consequences. Most likely, you will be forced to salvage your ship if the authorities think she is in the way of the shipping line…"

With a roar of the engines, the coast guards left us. Slowly, his words started to carry meaning in my mind; *They had two big pumps onboard, well enough to have kept Anna afloat until we reached port...*

Anna, a last look
(Photo: The Swedish coastguards)

Epilogue

In the town Borgholm, there was a small hostel called *Hotel Wilma*. Apparently, it used to be a refuge for the shipwrecked since the 1800's, welcoming anyone saved from the gruesome fate of drowning.

With hot broth and empathy, the owners embraced us – an old couple with extensive knowledge of how to take good care of unfortunate souls. In their "special room for the shipwrecked", we slowly returned to life without being disturbed and tried to recover from the surrealistic nightmare. The only exception being people from several newspapers calling and insisting on interviewing us. The day after, we could read the full story and see the featured pictures taken by the coast guards...

We stayed for two days, consistently in the caring embrace of the gentle landlord and his wife. He assured us that one of the most important means of mentally healing was to eat nourishing food accompanied by decent beer and quite a few shots of snaps.

He claimed, with emphasis:

"You see, my young lads, it will take away all evil and gloomy thoughts and bring you back to life!"

During the last night, he gathered us in front of the fireplace to tell us about his own adventures at sea. As it turned out, one of them featured another case of a whim of faith... Many years ago, him and his father owned a Baltic trader that was shipping sandstone from the island Öland to ports all around the Baltic Sea. I asked him about the name of the ship.

"Oh, she was a beautiful lady. A two masted schooner, rigged and with a reliable Hundested semi diesel... Her name was *Viking of Borgholm*."

He sighed with dreamy eyes:

"She sailed so well... And those were probably the best years of my life... I always wondered what happened to her..."

I could enlighten him and tell him of the adventures and sad fate of *The Spirit of Chicago*.

A couple of weeks later, I hired a professional diver to examine the wreck of my beautiful *Anna*. He reported back that her hull was cracked open and impossible to salvage. Of all the equipment onboard, he found nothing. He never sent me a bill.

I was haunted by the notion of having to remove the wreck, like the coast guards said. It would be a very costly endeavour that most likely would have made me bankrupt. I contacted the Swedish Maritime Authority to get my verdict. Somewhat surprised, they told me that they had never heard of such nonsense! In fact, no one had ever been required to remove a small wooden ship from the bottom of the sea...!

And so, finally, I got a good night's sleep.

A small comfort in all the misery was that *Anna* was fully insured to her full purchase value. I was going to be refunded, and thus retrieve my grandmother's legacy.

But a couple of months later, the insurance company International Insurance informed me that the insurance had not been transferred into my name at the time of the shipwreck and, therefore, they refused to pay me anything except for a symbolic sum of 4000 crowns (for the loss of my clothes) ...

The insurance fee was paid in advance, and I was assured that everything was in order. A lawyer friend and neighbour of mine got very upset and initiated a pro bono process to assist me. Unfortunately, he was in his 70s and died of a heart attack shortly after.

Finally, in all fairness, my experiences with the Swedish coast guard have been very positive. Well-motivated men and women patrol our coast, and they are doing a great job. The commander of TV 231 and his lack of judgement is long forgiven, and can only be regarded as an exception from an otherwise honourable professional corp.

Finally

An extra twist of this story appeared a while ago as I was working on the translation of this book. I was looking for information about the cargo ship *Susanne* and got in touch with a relative to the owner, who passed away many years ago. It turned out that he and his ship conducted advanced signals intelligence for the Swedish government/Secret Service...scanning the Baltic Sea for Soviet activities.

6th of June 1974 she most likely was on her way on a new mission when she came to our rescue. The captain was a known intelligence officer/spy at the time. *Susanne* later got sold and finally ended up in the Caribbean Sea. In 2005 she was removed from the Lloyds Registre.

M/S Susanne of Stockholm
(Photo: unknown)

TOR HELGE

One-time, kindred souls
they may be called, they who's track
you cross but once.
In the midst of life, they are gone,
and all that remains.
is the memory, the warmth, the scent, the laughter
and the gesture showing
how the albatross flies...

M/S Tor Helge
(Photo: the author)

Norwegian passenger- and postal boat/ferry launched in 1915 nearby Trondheim. Overall length: 22 meters. Beam: 5 meters. Built in the traditional Norwegian way, pine on pine. Equipped with a 2 cylinder 150 Hp semidiesel Brunvoll.

F all came early this year. A roaring storm from north-west turned every tree into naked watchers of a dark winter. My work as a sailmaker in Denmark came to an end for this season and, as usual, I went back to my other occupation of being a longshoreman in the port of Helsingborg. In those days, cargo ships looked like cargo ships, with old fashioned cargo hatches and loading masts.

In a never-ending line they arrived from far away ports, their cargo rooms loaded with fruit, coffee beans, copper, wine, iron fillings, electronics, just about everything you could imagine from all around the world. Anyone could get a job for a day or two if the foreman considered you to be healthy and able. By 6:30 in the morning I had to be ready and waiting in line for inspection at the docks, at which time the foreman would thoroughly examine the crowd of applicants. Anyone who was approved got a yellow note stating which ship to work on that day. In the days before container dominance, the work of a longshoreman was extremely taxing. All of the cargo had to be loaded and unloaded by hand, and every man feared the worst types: coffee beans in sacks of 75 kilograms or 20 kilograms of fruit in boxes, solidly packed by the vibrations emanating from the ship throughout the journey across the oceans.

I lucked out that fall and was offered work for several weeks, allowing me to save up some money. But one night in a deep cargo hold of the *S/S Star of India*, surrounded by diesel fumes and ridden with a terrible headache, I decided it was about time for another trip somewhere, for a new adventure. Antarctica was a tempting contender. In Martinique, I got acquainted with a French scientist that offered me a job on the French Antarctic station Dumont d'Urville. For some reason, there was a constant shortage of service, repair, and transport personnel, to name a few. My family and friends fiercely objected because people returning from Antarctica had become "introverted, grown long beards, and replaced their souls with icicles". Always receptive to sensible advice, I put my eventual Antarctic excursion on hold. But I had to go somewhere… The question was where – and how.

Late one night in October, the phone rang. On a crackling line, I heard an English voice:

"Hi Burger! It's Brad."

"Who?"

"Brad from *Carita* in Las Palmas! How's life?"

After a couple of seconds, I realised who he was:

"Bradley! Hello! I'm great. Where are you? In Canada?"

He laughed and replied:

"Copenhagen, Burg. Copenhagen."

Half an hour later, I knew why he was in Copenhagen. The whole Las Palmas crew of *Carita* (Bradley, Whayne, George and Michelle, Randy, and his girlfriend Beth), all my friends from the failed endeavour of crossing the Atlantic, had returned to Canada. There, they worked to save up money and return to Europe, hoping to find a ship of their own. In a remote fjord north of Trondheim, they found what they were looking for – a sixty-year-old postal boat/ferry, once in service between the isolated islands on the Norwegian Atlantic coast, carrying passengers, mail, and sheep. Twenty-two meters long and equipped with a two-cylinder hot-bulb Brunvoll semidiesel, gaff rigged with one mast.

"Quite a bargain!" he continued, and I could feel my heart beating faster.

"Would you consider joining us down to the Mediterranean? We are in need of a licensed skipper, at least until we reach southern Spain."

I thought about my recently finished and approved skipper's exam and immediately felt indispensable for the continuation of my friend's adventure.

He went on:

"You see, Burg, we intend on doing some charter sailing down there… And we would love for you to become a part owner! How about it…? Do you want to tag along?"

With Bradley still on the line, my left hand grabbed the knapsack from underneath the bed.

The ferry journey from Sweden to Denmark gives you just enough time for a herring sandwich and a Tuborg beer. The train from Helsingør to Copenhagen was filled with cigar smoking commuters and took 30 minutes. After that, I jumped in a cab to clear the final stretch to the commercial port of Copenhagen. The morning fog dispersed, and, at the far end of a pier, I spotted a black ship with one mast and a slightly oversized superstructure. I began contemplating my imminent captain duties of a ship named *Tor Helge,* a man's name… I found comfort in the fact that the Norwegians often gave their ships male titles and not female ones. Why should it be necessary to travel the seas on a "her"? But, while writing this story, for my own piece of mind, I will refer to the ship as a "her".

To claim she was beautiful would be… a bit of a stretch. But she had rare slim lines, a straight bow, and a nicely rounded stern. With her quite high centre of gravity, she tended to always tilt a bit, regardless of the efforts put into balancing her out.

But she turned out to be a seaworthy vessel, buoyant and steady as a rock under any conditions.

My thoughts were interrupted by my friends swarming the deck, heartedly greeting me, and filling me in on any news before taking me for a tour around the ship.

In Copenhagen
(Photo: the author)

Filled by a sensation of happiness and excitement, I knew this was the right place to be! *Tor Helge* radiated the right amount of romantic adventure and unpredictability that I yearned for, helping me to forget the sad ending of my *Anna*. The rest of the day, I helped out with buying more equipment and food for the trip. I was to share a cabin with Brad and Whayne, situated just aft of the engine room and above the propeller shaft. The sleeping quarters (stacked like boxes along the ship's side), were 1.80 by 0.60 metres and had a headroom of 50 centimetres, cleverly made for sleeping sailors not to be thrown out in heavy seas. On the downside, it was just as difficult to get in or out of them during calm seas. There were no port holes this close to the water line, just a small inspection hatch connecting the cabin to the engine room.

The staircase leading to deck was so narrow that you were forced to take a deep breath and squeeze your shoulders together to climb it.

The ingenious construction of a cabin made for humans being placed right above the propeller shaft, only separated from the engine by a thin wooden wall, gave me a newfound appreciation for earplugs; not to keep the noise out, but to reduce most of the high-pitched whooshing sounds emanating from the propeller and generator. The fumes of diesel and lubrication oil were even harder to cope with, even though I sort of like the smell of it – a scent associated with the sea. But, when I discovered that any beverage immediately became covered with a layer of oil, me and my cabin mates decided to remove the cabin door and drill several ventilation holes in the ceiling bordering to the saloon above. The cabin was a stinking hellhole, but we had to live with it and, whenever the sea was calm, we slept in the aft saloon.

Early the next morning, we cast off and headed south. Randy, who was not used to the sea at all and a bit anxious (about pretty much everything), demanded that we stay inshore as much as possible, thus using the Kiel Canal and keeping inside of the Frisian Islands, above the Wadden Sea and the IJsselmeer, while heading towards Amsterdam. After crossing the English Channel headed down to Plymouth, we awaited good weather for our crossing between Land's End and Cape Finisterre. A moderate, westerly breeze allowed us to hoist the mainsail and jib, making good headway towards Møns Klint. The October sky cleared and gave way to a warming sun. As we were not on watch, me and Brad got comfortable on the aft deck and enjoyed a couple of beers, tucking us into a peaceful slumber.

Randy's hollering brusquely awoke us:

"You've got to come! Michelle is sick, something is wrong with her mouth!"

In the saloon, we found Michelle stretched out on one of the benches, moaning and crying, apparently in great pain. Her left cheek was red and swollen. George tried to keep calm:

"She had a wisdom tooth removed in Copenhagen and was supposed to get rid of the stitches before we left … but we forgot all about it…"

Everyone except for Whayne, who was at the helm, were gathered around the patient.

"You mean you've still got the stitches?" Michelle nodded in anguish.

"When did she go to the dentist?"

George stared at the floor and mumbled:

"Maybe 14 days ago … or so…" Suddenly he raised his head, his worried expression now replaced by a big smile.

"Burg! I just remembered! You're some kind of medical orderly, right? Could you please have look at her?"

I was just beginning to get my sea legs back but could feel a faint wave of nausea come over me, intermingled with burps tasting of beer. I nodded, carefully sat her up, and had her open her mouth. An acrid gust of breath hit me.

"I need a flashlight!" Her oral cavity was a disaster, swollen and stinking of pus. Where the tooth had previously been, I could spot three stitches, barely visible. My nausea grew.

"As I see it, we've got two options: either head for the closest port and get her to a hospital … or…" the four of them stared at me in desperation, whereas Michelle had passed out and was breathing heavily, "…or someone must remove the stitches right away. But, in any case, she has to see a doctor!"

George ran off but was back in a flash carrying a well-supplied first-aid bag.

In awe, I studied the contents: scissors, scalpels, bandages, salt tablets, ascorbic acid, disinfection fluid, antibiotic pills. A neat case contained suture needles and a bottle of catgut and, at the very bottom, there was a small, sealed plastic box marked with a U.S. Army label.

"What's this?"

"Morphine, for emergencies only…" Randy replied.

"Well equipped bag, this…" I mumbled while changing the wet towel on Michelle's head. I could feel the taste of breakfast bacon in my throat, working its way back up.

"How to do this…" I mumbled and, in an instant, I knew what I had to do. The rest of the crew had placed themselves at a safe distance from the coming ordeal, with reassuring expressions on their faces that read: "We're here in the background, ready to assist you at any moment." Yeah, right…

Bradley gave me a pat on the back and went upstairs to the bridge to assist Randy with, if necessary, finding a suitable port. I swallowed hard and cursed my exaggerated fame as a ship's doctor.

"Is this something you really want me to do, Michelle?" She answered with a slight nod, closed her eyes, and opened her mouth.

Tor Helge heaved softly and regularly in the swell. By bracing myself with one foot under a radiator, I carefully eased the scissors (a bit too big and blunt) underneath the first stitch, but every movement made Michelle moan in agony. At last, with the help of a wooden spatula, I managed to cut the first stich. A quick snap and pull with the surgical pliers and it was out! Now that I had gotten the hang of it, the rest of them were easy to pull out. However, the foul odour in her mouth and the heave of the sea made me dizzy and close to throwing up. One task remained.

"Beth, can you please get some stuff for me? A lemon, a bottle of mineral water, and a bucket … and the bottle of Aquavit I brought onboard … but be quick, please!" She was quick. I cut the lemon in half and squeezed it into half a glass of water. In small sips, I drank this excellent remedy for nausea.

"Now then, Michelle. You must endure a little bit more pain for a couple of seconds … I have to squeeze out as much of the pus as possible … and it's going to hurt a bit…" She opened her mouth. With tweezers lined with Aquavit-soaked cotton, I got to work. Carefully, I placed each end of the tweezers onto the dentin and made a firm, quick squeeze. Michelle's body formed an arch as my fingers sunk into her gums, our joint howl drowning every other sound of the ship – the loud engine, the ever-rattling vending machine, and every other miscellaneous noise. Beth threw me the bucket and, a second later, Michelle relieved herself of the blood-mixed pus.

The very next moment, I threw up by the leeward railing. Back in the saloon, Michelle was sitting up, rinsing out her mouth and spitting with a huge grin on her face.

"If you lay down just once more, I will check if there is more to come out... It's important, you see..." She interrupted me, narrowed her dark, French Moroccan eyes, and growled:

"Touch me again and I'll kill you!"

A relieved laughter filled the saloon of *Tor Helge*. George, who had remained dead silent during the ordeal, raised his voice:

"Baby... Please rinse your mouth out with the Aquavit ... and then, my friends, we'll all have us some of that strong stuff! Especially you, Burg!"

Michelle's pain disappeared right away and, after few days on antibiotics, she was fully recovered.

In the evening, the fog returned, and we kept our course across the Great Belt, heading straight towards Kiel Bay. Around midnight, me and Brad got ready to take our turn at the helm, relieving Randy and Beth.

Brad studied the chart and asked:

"What's our current position?"

"Right here... I think..." said Randy, pointing south of Langeland.

"Think...?" Brad was hot tempered, but attempted to control his rage as he continued:

"For fucks sake, you must have written down any changes to the course ... otherwise you haven't a clue of where we are!"

"I know we're here ... period," he replied, let go of the helm, and disappeared down the stairs.

Brad was outraged. We reduced the speed and considered our options. Finally, we decided on a south by southwest course and put the radar on its maximum range, helping us in spotting several echoes from ships most likely on their way in or out of Kiel. At the end of our watch, we could discern distant lights coming from our destination. With all hands on deck, we moored along a German pier.

The future charter yacht, *Tor Helge*, was to be supplied with a voluminous stock of miscellaneous liquor in order to please future charter customers. Being aware of my ship mates' drinking habits, I had my doubts about this. After we had eaten breakfast the following morning, a local ship's chandler was contacted. With a rubicund face and a twisted handlebar moustache he appeared and, refusing to come onboard, received our order from the pier:

"Ten boxes of Johnny Walker, Black Label, and..." Whayne cleared his throat and continued:

"Three cases of Bacardi white rum, and four cases of Beefeater's gin ... that makes a total of 324 bottles..."

Even though a bottle of Johnny Walker only set us back 15 Swedish crowns in those days, this made a considerable dent in the ship's funds. Since half of our common resources were about to be spent, I made a modest proposal of perhaps excluding some of the liquor.

My suggestion was met with disgruntled faces and my proposition turned down. The Kiel canal was not only expensive, but also a long and boring passage culminating in the town of Brunsbüttel, right by the North Sea. We moored just behind the last lock alongside three rusty barges. Getting ashore proved to be a risky task, balancing on a narrow span right above pointy iron beams. The evening brought a warm and mild wind as well as a scent of the North Sea from the other side of the embarkments, the very same waters from which *Tor Helge* came, her home waters of Hitra, Vega and Dønna on the Norwegian west coast.

Right across from us, on the northern shore of the canal, we spotted a beautiful two-masted ship. I immediately identified it as a Colin Archer design.

The Mermaid
(Photo unknown, postcard)

We decided to pay them a visit after dinner. George and Michelle were occupying the galley this evening and exquisite fumes found its way out onto deck. The last of the canned meat got transformed into a culinary feast. This turned out to be the second to last enjoyable dinner onboard. The financial status among my friends was far worse than they had told me and, from now on, we had to maintain a meagre menu: coffee, hard rye bread, condensed milk, mustard, raspberry jam, potatoes, canned peas and, finally, a mountain of canned "somethings" without labels. Whayne proudly declared that he had gotten his hands on a huge stock of cans, supposedly containing fish and meat. The ship's chandler assured him that it was all high-quality food and, although unlabelled, they were all still "first class".

The truth was revealed as we continued our journey; all cans contained a variety of fishcakes, fish-balls, and fish-pudding. I will refrain from trying to depict our unsuccessful attempts at ennobling these disgusting meals.

After dinner, all of us except Randy and Beth went for a stroll to inspect the fine ship across the harbor. *The Mermaid* was her name, artistically carved onto her bows. A blond, crew-cut head of hair appeared in the hatch, followed by a pair of ice blue eyes suspiciously staring at us.

"Nice ship, it's really something," I mumbled, whereupon the man stepped out on deck and invited us onboard. With a handshake as forcefully constricting as a carpenter's vice, he presented himself as Ernst. With his recently purchased *Mermaid,* him and his crew, a retired submarine captain, were on their way to Venezuela. A military degree of order prevailed onboard. Everything was in perfect symmetry, organised and seemed to "stand in attention". This boat was, by all accounts, the most optimal vessel I had ever come across. Sixty feet long with a hull made entirely of whole two-inch teak planking from stem to stem. Everything onboard was made to withstand a hurricane. Two gaff-rigged masts, an inner and outer jib, and a giant square-sail. Brass, bronze and shiny layers of varnish, every detail in perfect condition.

Ernst ended the guided tour by inviting us to join him for a drink in the saloon, furnished with dark mahogany and black oak. An exquisite, suspended table was surrounded by dark blue, plush sofas. Wagner's "Ride of the Valkyries" played out of invisible speakers, amassing a strange and somewhat unsettling feeling.

The submarine captain was leaning over a chart table and greeted us with a silent nod. He had a fascinating quality – not only due to the fact that he was wearing the submariner's cap carried by all WWII submarine captains, but also due to the air of opposition he still maintained against the cruel reality that made his side loose the battle on the Atlantic. Uneasily, I wondered how many sailors lives he had ended…

As if he had read my mind, Ernst stated:

"My friend Claus here has had 32 confirmed sinkings..." he made a pause and smiled:

"And many more unconfirmed..." Ernst did not even try to hide his admiration for this predator. Soon, the table was set with Brandy and Stroh Rhum, and Claus was serving huge drinks in crystal glasses. When he reached across the table, part of his sweater lifted above the waist of his trousers, revealing a gun holstered on the inside of his belt. Unsurprisingly, I could ascertain that it was a Luger Po 8, the most common sidearm used by the officers in the Wehrmacht and Kriegsmarine during the war. My initial feeling of comfort was quickly replaced by panic. Why the hell was he armed? Were we being hijacked? The thought was absurd, no one got hijacked or kidnapped on a Thursday night in Brunsbüttel. Maybe these guys were just fans of guns, appealed by the feeling of a cold Luger stuffed inside of their belt. Besides, many sailing yachts carried arms onboard, shotguns, calibre 22s, and such.

You can run into pirates in different places of the world, and many deep blue sailors insist on the necessity of being armed, stating that the mere sight of a weapon will scare the bad guys away. I was, and am, sceptical towards this. Also, an American gentleman once told me that if I choose to fire a gun at someone, I had better make it fatal, or I could risk being sued...

The crew of *Tor Helge* kept a reserved, yet polite attitude throughout the evening, but as the contents of the bottles started disappearing, the toasts became merrier and more frequent. I worried about our approaching departure, set to take place at 08:00 a.m. the following morning. We shared our plans for the Mediterranean, but they did not share much in return of their plans in Venezuela. Ernst told us about his military background (not surprising), and his involvement in miscellaneous business ventures, which had been successful. His dream was to sail to South America to implement his new business deals, of which he revealed nothing. He came across *The Mermaid* by accident and bought her off an elderly English couple for 100,000 D-Mark. As he was not a seafarer, he wisely hired a professional, Claus. In Ernst's opinion, the most skilled sailor money could buy.

As the evening passed, it became clear to me that Ernst and Claus had extremely far right political views and opinions. Shady statements dating back to the '30s were being presented as solutions for today's world problems, only barely disguised by a veil of heartiness.

It was nearing midnight and George, still reasonably sober, suggested that it was about time for us to return to our ship. Ernst looked at us, one by one, with hazy eyes and exclaimed:

"Kameraden… After this evening I have come to realise that we are all brothers… Not brothers in arms … yet, but brothers ready to stand together!" He made a theatrical pause and gazed out through the skylight, got up from the coach, raised his glass, and pompously declared:

"I have decided to, as a sign of trust, show you my cabin!" He made it sound like a favour granted for the lucky few. Bradley had fallen asleep with a firm grip of his cognac glass, but George, Michelle, Whayne, and I accepted his generous invitation and followed Ernst to the forward cabin. The shock made us freeze right there, in the doorway. The cabin was not a cabin. It was an armoury. In perfect rows along the bulkheads, there were Schmeisser machine guns, Kalashnikovs, mortars, and Luger pistols. In bunches like overfed ticks, American hand grenades. Hanging from the roof, a heavy German machine gun from WWII, the greatly feared MG 42. Secured onto the floor, cases of ammunition.

"Now you're impressed!" Ernst held onto a cluster of gasmasks, puffed on his cigar, and continued:

"These, my new friends, are my tools! With all this, I will succeed in South America!" In a low, intimate voice he added:

"We'll see who gets the last laugh!"

German MG 42 from WWII
(Photo: unknown)

The crew of *Tor Helge*, now completely sober, all smiled synchronously while feeling the urge to quickly get off this ship from hell, preferably alive. Cautiously, I asked:

"Will it be safe to make port in Maracaibo with this cargo...?" Wrong thing to say. Briskly, he showed us out of the cabin and slammed the door.

"You can find your own way out!" he hissed and disappeared into the fo'c'sle.

Claus, once again leaning over the chart table, ignored us as we barely succeeded in levering Bradley up and out on deck. But fate had some more in store for us that night. Bradley was drunk, bordering on unconscious. We carried him over to our side of the canal. The 30-centimetre wide, half-rotten gangplank leading across the deadly barges, leaned slightly upwards. Beneath it the sharp, rusty beams posed a lethal threat to anyone who lost their balance. Having more than one person pass this abyss at a time was out of the question. Some sort of lifting or supporting gear had to be made if we were not going to leave Brad sleeping outside. What if he woke up and decided to wabble onboard by himself? We had just gotten away from a neo-Nazi ship alive, just to face a near impossible logistical problem. Preoccupied with contemplating this challenge, no one noticed that Bradley had silently awoken and begun heading straight for disaster, determined to make it back to his cosy bunk. For a couple of frightful seconds, it seemed like he was going to, against all odds, defy the laws of gravity and make it over. Then, suddenly, with only a few steps left, he stopped, fell asleep, and walked out into thin air. With a horrible thud, he hit the iron reinforced beams three meters down, by the water. For a sober person, a deadly fall. But, stood paralysed, we all witnessed the wonder of Brad getting back up on his feet, shrugging his head, and uttering the words that, from then on, became a mantra:

"What the hell am I doing down here...?"

Apart from a ring bolt imprint and a blueish nose, he was unharmed.

Later that afternoon, we finally got through the locks, steered across the outlet of the river Elbe, and made port in Cuxhaven. Since the weather was all right, Randy agreed to pass by the East Friesian Islands and sneak into the Dutch waters by Schiermonnikoog, the most northerly of the West Friesian Islands. At Terschelling, we cleared customs and got our liquor cargo thoroughly sealed. The customs official made it absolutely clear that, if we wished to avoid facing heavy fines and prison, the seals must not be broken until we reached international waters.

Passing Ameland, we understood the difficulties and hazards of navigating Dutch waters. High and low tides along with shifting winds made the sandy reefs move around in unpredictable patterns. The result was treacherous, winding waterways, constantly changing, temporarily marked by tree branches. To add insult to injury, no chart had been purchased for this passage, leaving us to rely on the *Shell Automobile Atlas*. At a waterway intersection, we were caught up by a heavily loaded barge on its way to Amsterdam. It passed by pretty closely, which made its skipper catch on to our situation and wave, indicating that we should follow him. A great idea, apart from the fact that he made better speed than us and slowly got further and further away. Despite our full throttle we could not keep up and, in the fading daylight, it became more and more difficult to see on which side of the sea markers the barge passed. Randy called out from the wheelhouse:

"Did anyone see on which side he passed that marker...?" He pointed at the next pole, just a few 100 metres ahead of us. No one had an answer. With giant leaps, George threw himself up the wheelhouse ladder and reversed the engine.

"Port side!" Whayne shouted, but Randy misunderstood and turned hard to starboard. Making nine knots, *Tor Helge* softly slid up onto the sand bank as the stern lantern of the barge *Wilma of Amsterdam* disappeared into the distance.

Low tide had begun. In pure despair, we watched the outgoing current make Waddenzee even more shallow. It did not have to end in disaster. If the boat stayed upright and did not keel over too much, we would not get stuck in the mud and sand. If we did get stuck, however, we might get flooded once the tide shifted, and the sea came rushing in. I yelled to George and Randy on the bridge:

"Reverse the propeller and give her full throttle!"

"What?"

"Full back!"

With *Tor Helge's* enormous propeller, we had a chance to dig ourselves out, shovelling the sand forward. There was a risk of ruining the cooling water pump, but it was a risk worth taking. Besides, we had a spare one. After five minutes of violent shaking of the hull, George stopped. She had not moved an inch but was still upright... Chances were that she had only gotten stuck by the bow. And I had noticed a slight movement of the stern.

"There's no use... Everything is just going to hell!" Beth had tears in her eyes and disappeared under deck. Brad and Whayne stomped back and forth, uttering every curse word they knew and using the foulest language they could think of. I had been in this situation before, and I knew it could work.

"Let's have another go at it, Brad! Let's move everything heavy back to the stern – anchors, oil drums, etc ... and all of us too!" The weight shifting could make a huge difference.

157

Michelle shouted to George in the wheelhouse:

"Once again. Full back!"

Like a steam train, flaming flakes of soot poured out of the exhaust and swirled away towards Texel and Vlieland. Almost unnoticeably, *Tor Helge* freed herself from the sand bank. In her sudden freedom, she almost ran aground on the other side of the narrow waterway. George struggled fiercely with the wheel and controls, but eventually got the ship back on its course again. The rest of the way to Afsluitdijk had been wisely marked in a way that no one could misinterpret, with branches that were closer together. And the cooling water pump was unharmed.

At midnight, we passed the lock into the manmade Lake IJssel. In their never-ending struggle for more land, the Dutch managed to accomplish the impossible by fending off parts of the North Sea, pumping the water out, and turning the former seabed into fields of tulips and tomatoes. IJsselmeer, a place where mighty East India ships once anchored, is now forever closed off from the North Sea and most probably will remain a lake, as politicians and environmental groups argue about its future.

With less than six inches of water under our keel, we travelled the remaining miles to Amsterdam and moored at 04:00 a.m. in the middle of the city, right next to trams, neon lights and heavy traffic. In this the capital of pleasures and flowers, we encountered the beautiful Swedish ketch *Patria,* on her way home after spending three years in the Mediterranean Sea.

One night, on a whim of economical madness, we went to a restaurant just to get a break from our fish pudding menu, spending the worth of about 1000 litres of diesel.

After anguished consideration, we realised the necessity of quickly getting on our way again. The ship's coffer could not handle anymore exuberance. The day after, we headed out through the canal to IJmuiden, the last lock before the open sea.

A raging storm pulled in from north-west. Monstrous, breaking waves filled the air with salty foam, covering both *Tor Helge* and the lock guards. A day later, the wind died down and we dared to enter the English Channel, with our course set for Rotterdam. The wisest decision would probably have been to keep our course outside the Dutch islands and only make port when necessary, but my Canadian friends were determined to practice total democracy. Randy suffered, not only from sea sickness, but also from fear of the sea, thereby demanding that we head south while staying as close as possible to dry land. So, we took the inshore waterways via canals across the river Scheldt to Rotterdam, and out to sea again by Vlissingen.

Approaching Rotterdam is somewhat depressing, going through industrial fog and polluted waters, the only mooring sites being alongside dirty quays cluttered with containers and trucks.

What took place over the following three days became a determining factor for my contemplation of signing off as captain and returning home. It all started with the fact that one of our main batteries had died. It was long overdue its natural life span and refused to be charged, whereas the ship's coffer did not allow for any investments whatsoever. The few dollars remaining were just barely going to last to Gibraltar and would even then only be enough for buying food and fuel. George came up with a plan… My protesting, taking place during supper as we feasted on another tin of "Fishcake Surprise", was in vain.

George's voice was filled with compassion as he addressed me:

- "Nobody likes this Burg, but what else can we do? We must regard it as an emergency loan…"

"Emergency loan," I cried, "that's an amusing nickname for thieving… I've never heard that one before!"

"It probably won't affect anyone poor…" Beth whispered, and Whayne, while refilling our whisky glasses, rounded it all off by submitting:

"Besides, all these guys have insurance, so ... no harm done!"

"I'm going to bed," I mumbled, and left them to their conspiring.

It so happened that a freshly awoken French lorry driver found that his batteries had gone through severe ageing the morning after. In a silent air of guilty remorse and drizzling rain, *Tor Helge* continued its voyage across the winding Scheldt River delta. By that afternoon, we reached the Western Scheldt, which is the actual outlet of that mighty river. During its 400-kilometre passage towards the sea, it had passed three countries – France, Belgium, and Holland – collecting enormous quantities of water which, when it meets the westerly winds of the sea, creates very unpleasant short waves. Especially for small Norwegian postal ferries. The canal between Yerseke (where they by the way make an excellent Bisque d'Homard) and Krabbendijke did not take long and had a small, westerly gale. *Tor Helge* steamed westward as usual, with a five-degree tilt. George and Michelle were at the helm and, every now and then, a hazy sun broke through the chasing clouds. Scheldt's muddy waters irregularly broke over the ship's bow. Randy suffered from severe seasickness and got cared for by Beth down in the fo'c'sle. Brad was in the galley, trying to magically transform the upcoming dinner, and Whayne had gone to sleep in our dungeon. As for myself, I had curled up under a tarpaulin on foredeck, reading about the last voyage of the barque Herzogin Cecilie. As a continuous routine, we used to check the engine every half hour. A semidiesel engine is very reliable and just keeps on running, causing very little trouble, but it must be lubricated regularly. Also, there are several greasing spots that must be refilled and tightened. I watched as George headed down to the engine room but, all of a sudden, he came rushing back out on yelling:

"Fire! There is a fire! The whole engine is burning!" I immediately saw the white smoke pouring out from the open engine room door. In seconds, everyone was on deck. Michelle, at the helm, put the engine in idle and closed the throttle.

"Keep her up wind"! I shouted, and our ship slowed down and came to a full stop. Brad tied a wet towel around his head and went down to the engine. Thirty seconds later, he was back on deck and hissed, between cough attacks:

"I can't see any fire…! It's like a dark hell down there!"

Whayne took a deep breath and went downstairs but returned right away:

"Just a shitload of smoke down there… and hot as a stove!"

In my head, I feverishly tried to come up with an answer to what could be the cause. Had it been the batteries, the fumes would have been lethal, and Brad would never have made it back up on deck. If the fuel was burning, we would see the flames and be piling ourselves into the life rafts by now.

I silently mumbled to myself:

"The generator…"

Then, at the top of my lungs, I yelled:

"The generator! Michelle, shut down the engine!" Her black head of hair peaked out of the wheelhouse window:

"Quoi?" When exposed to stressful situations, she had a habit of reverting back into the French language.

"The engine! Shut down the engine!" My voice broke into a hoarse wheeze, and I accidently swallowed my snuff.

"D'accord," she yelled back, and the hot bulb died out with a final sigh of the chimney. Paralysed, standing outside the engine room door, we watched as the dark Gehenna smoke slowly began clearing up. *Tor Helge* was still gently riding against the wind, with no immediate lee shore in sight. I felt the aftermath of the swallowed snuff and had to feed the fishes from the railing. From the engine room, I could hear George's voice:

"Shit, Burger, you were right!"

The generator had jammed, but the three sturdy generator belts kept wearing, creating violent friction and heavy smoke. We removed the belts, prised the big flywheel into position, and the Brunvoll started up again like nothing had happened.

Way down south-west, we spotted the small fishing village Terneuzen, a suitable port for the repairs and overhaul we needed to do. Since we had a spare generator, this incident would not delay us more than a couple of hours.

The port was a bit too shallow for our ship, so we moored on the outside of an old palisade at the end of the pier. To encourage the crew, George promised to arrange for a lavish dinner that day, a statement that made us all wonder if he had inhaled too much smoke. Wearing his oversized oil coat, he giddily took off to go shopping.

The new generator was installed quickly and worked perfectly but, as the hours went by, we regrettably decided on staying overnight. George returned after an hour, but we could immediately see that there was something wrong with his appearance. His meagre nature had changed. Strange tumours could be discerned under his coat, misshaping his otherwise slender appearance. He gathered the crew of *Tor Helge* in the saloon, and, with his most charming smile, he opened his coat and revealed what was inside. A collective roar emerged from all of us. The sight was irresistible. George had committed another "emergency loan" and I finally gave up on my friend's sense of honesty. In the lining of his coat, there were two fresh chickens, a giant pack of French fries, ketchup, a red Edam cheese, and a paper bag filled with lukewarm baguettes. From his bottomless pockets, he hauled up three bottles of red wine.

How he had managed to successfully steal a substantial dinner for seven people is, to this day, a mystery. But I did eat with a hearty appetite and suppressed my bad conscience by way of the excellent wine. The taste of Norwegian canned fishcakes could no longer be improved with strawberry jam or mustard, and we all yearned for a decent meal.

162

This fatal day could have ended with an "all's well onboard". A fed, slumbering crew boldly getting up the next day and preparing themselves for the English Channel. But, once more, fate had something else in store for us. While enjoying our morning coffee, a polite voice reached us from the pier:

"Customs…"

The messy dinner table from last night had been cleared, and there were no traces of our chicken orgy to be discovered.

"No one sends the customs to arrest shop lifters… this must be a routine check…" went through my head. Indeed, it was. Together with Michelle, one of the officials went under deck to look around while the other one checked our passports and ship documents. Everybody smiled with relief as they realised that this was a normal procedure, expected to take place in any foreign port. Afterwards, the crew of *Tor Helge* only suffered from minor bad conscience. Randy, however, had turned pale and withdrew to the far end of the pier. The official from below deck appeared and uttered with a stern voice:

"Can I please have another look at the admission documents?" Whayne opened the brief case and handed over the list of custom cleared bottles of liquor, duly stamped by the customs officer in Terschelling.

"There are 324 bottles registered here…" he moved his spectacles down to the tip of his nose, making his appearance a little less strict.

"Yes… and?" Whayne's smile froze.

"There are two bottles missing in the sealed compartment."

George stepped forward and said:

"Impossible! None of us have been near that compartment… it was properly sealed!"

"Nevertheless, there are two bottles missing … please go down and check for yourselves!" The crew of *Tor Helge* squeezed into the fo'c'sle. The seal had been opened by the customs officer and everyone could see that a box of Johnny Walker had been

163

opened. Every box contained 12 bottles, in this one only 10 were left. On the panelling beneath the cupboard, there were scratch marks with two boards loose. Inside was an empty space with its ceiling bordering to the liquor compartment… and another board loose. But who could be responsible?

Randy was still on the pier, pacing back and forth, smoking. He did not have to admit to anything, the guilt was written all over his face. In despair, we all gathered on deck, aware of the imminent threat of consequences. With tears in his eyes, Randy tried to explain himself; whisky was the only remedy for his seasickness… he just did not have the strength to resist the temptation!

"Who is the captain onboard?" The officials buttoned up their uniforms, as to emphasize the seriousness of the situation. One of them continued without waiting for an answer:

"In accordance with paragraph 18 of the Dutch sea regulations, you will be charged with violating Dutch law concerning the import and transport of customs cleared goods within Dutch territorial waters. Evidently, two bottles have been removed from the sealed compartment on this ship's passage between Terschelling and Terneuzen in Dutch waters. A few seconds of silence followed before a shrill voice could be heard from the pier above:

"Him, there … he's, our captain!" Randy's finger was pointed right at me, and the officials turned around to face me, the only Swede onboard.

We had all agreed to keep my captain's status to ourselves and only use it for qualification inquiries, since this ship required a licensed skipper. The owners were to take collective responsibility in case of trouble. With a firm grip on my arms, I was taken away to a waiting black car. My feelings during this moment are difficult to mediate – I did not fear the inside of a Dutch prison, but the uncertainty of what was going to happen was very unpleasant.

The prison bunk was not all that uncomfortable, and the food was excellent. After a short interrogation, I was told that the hearing would take place the day after.

I fell asleep early and slept better than I had done for a long time. The delicious breakfast contributed to brightening my somewhat gloomy situation. The hearing began at 10:00 a.m., after George and Brad had been picked up from the ship. This made me feel better. The thought had crossed my mind, aware of my friends' unconventional view of what was right or wrong, that they might have tried to make a run for it in the dead of night, leaving their skipper to pine away in a Dutch prison. But they arrived, and we went through it together. After a brief summary, the verdict was presented: a total fine of 1000 Guilders and a forfeit of all the liquor onboard. If the fine was not paid in full within 24 hours, captain Sjoberg was to be sentenced to a minimum of three months' imprisonment. The judge's club landed on the desk with a bang, and I was brought back to my cell.

The following night was not as pleasant. My worries returned. The crew of *Tor Helge* were still my friends, all except for Randy, perhaps. I could not imagine them taking off without me, refusing to pay the fine. International waters were not far away... 1000 Guilder represented more than half of the ship's coffer and could result in a sad ending of their adventure. George had hinted that his uncle in Manitoba expressed a wish to invest in *Tor Helge*, but only as an absolute last, emergency resort.

The morning of had arrived, and I woke up early from a restless slumber. Not even breakfast cheered me up. The hours went by without anyone from the ship showing up. The officials from yesterday came by, glanced at me, and shook their heads in pity. My thoughts shifted between hope and despair, but settled once I decided that I could endure three months in prison and keep in touch with my family back home by sending them letters.

Four o'clock in the afternoon, I heard steps in the corridor. Everyone but Randy and Beth had arrived, excited and happy. Bradley was waving a thick bundle of Guilder bills around, and we all embraced. I got to hear all about what had unfolded during my time behind bars. Money had arrived from Canada, and they never had the idea of escaping in the dead of night (a possibility the customs must have considered, since an armed coast guard cruiser had moored outside *Tor Helge*, making any escape impossible). Onboard, another trial had taken place, an emotional and furious showdown. I was not informed in detail on what had occurred but, judging by Randy's blue eye, the matter was considered settled. Part of his penance was to ask me for forgiveness, resulting in many hugs, tears, and sincere remorse.

Four sturdy officials unloaded all the liquor and carried them onboard the coast guard cruiser. There was not a dry eye. A small fortune in gin, whiskey, and rum was forever gone. The cruisers double V-8 engines started up and they began to cast off. I could not restrain myself and shouted to the commander:

"Enjoy!" A hearty smile appeared on his face, and he turned to a sailor and issued a command. The moment after, the sailor handed over a box of Johnny Walker Black Label, containing seven bottles.

"One for each of you ..." he saluted, and they took off towards Vlissingen, just as the sun set.

Epilogue

I had made the decision to sign off in Oostende, Belgium. It had taken more time than we had planned to get this far, and I had to return to my job as a longshoreman. The distance to Oostende only took us a few hours, where we moored at a calm spot in the inner harbor. I stayed onboard for a couple of days, and we had a relaxing time exploring the Belgian alehouses, enjoying the fantastic Belgian Trappist beer, a very strong beverage best consumed with moderation. After two or three bottles, you may be too far gone.

So, I left my Canadian friends – a bunch of likeable, humorous, and loveable people. We had experienced some memorable adventures together, and I always wondered what had happened to them after we parted, as I never heard from them again. According to a rumour, they had made it to Gibraltar but skipped the Mediterranean and made their way over to the West Indies.

As for *Tor Helge*, the old lady from the Tröndelags coast in Norway, I hope she is still afloat.

As for the beautiful Colin Archer *"The Mermaid"* she probably never reached South America with her cargo of deadly weapons and was abandoned near Ibiza in the Mediterranean. In 1978, she was found, in a very poor shape, by some Norwegian businesspeople that fortunately recognized her as a very important part of the Norwegian maritime heritage. She was brought back to Norway and restored to her original splendour and renamed *"Wyvern"* In 1987 she was handed over to the Stavanger Maritime Museum.

A few years ago, she was shipwrecked while sailing in the Baltic Sea but salvaged and once again restored.

The fate of Claus and Ernst remains a mystery.

S/Y Wyvern today
(Photo: Stavanger Maritime Museum)

To Whom it May Concern,

I can personally recomend Birger Sjöberg of Helsingborg, Sweden to skipper any persons ship. He served on my vessel M/S "TOR HELGE" as captain for three months. We experienced some difficult times sailing the North Sea during the winter months of 1974. At all times I found that Birger handled himself very professionally. His knowledge of rigging helped me enormously.

MS "TOR HELGE" - LHMF   Ship owner's
48 gross tonnage   George Harris
Canadian registry   TORONTO, CANADA.

TORONTO, CANADA.

TORONTO

TERJE OF TJØTTA

"The cure for anything is salt water: sweat, tears, or the sea."

—Karen Blixen

F/V Terje av Tjötta
(Photo: the author)

Northland pine on pine "shark" launched in Sandnessjøen, Norway in 1924. Length: 14 metres. Beam: 3.5 metres. Originally outfitted with sail and motor, 35 HP Rap semidiesel with a maximum rpm of 345. A typical Norwegian fishing boat, mainly used for fishing in the vicinity of Lofoten.

T his story is dedicated to all the kind and helpful people along the Norwegian Atlantic coast that made sure a couple crazy Swedes returned home in one piece.

We spotted her there, anchored in a sheltered bay by the small village Tjötta, not far from the Arctic Circle. For 50 years, she brought her bounty home from the Norwegian Sea; halibut, cod, salmon, and shark. Every spring, the motor was started up and did not get turned off until five months later, when the winter frost covered the pastures and mountains of the Helgeland coast. From then on, she could recover, moored by her home bay, awaiting the spring.

In the fading light of the setting sun, and in the shadow of the mighty mountain range The Seven Sisters, she was resting from a harsh life on Vestfjorden. It was a well-earned ease, she was retired and expected to perish where she was once built.

In lieu of this, she scarcely noticed the Swedish voices echoing from land...

Ship's logbook kept from May to June in 1976 on the voyage with *F/V Terje of Tjøtta* between the Arctic Circle and the west coast of Sweden:

May 27

Terje has been paid for in full – 14,000 Norwegian crowns have been handed over to the brothers Herlof and Erling at the farm Svinnes!

We left for Bergvågen's slip in the afternoon. All is well onboard, but we are only making two knots. Her hull is overgrown with seaweed. The crew onboard includes my fiancé Ie, Per, Jan, and myself. Erling and Herlof are tagging along for a bit as well, they are showing us the way to the wharf. After a perfect docking, the brothers threw themselves into their little dinghy and left us in a hurry...

At sunset we were pulled up onto the slipway.

We forgot to bring mattresses.

May 28

The hull is incredibly overgrown with barnacles and seaweed. The loose keel has been completely consumed by seaworms and needed to be changed, so the shipwright replaced it right away. Tomorrow we are doing another antifoul, and then we are going back into the water! The weather is fantastic and the sunsets here are amazing. We have a feeling this trip will be awesome. Bought a walker log and used charts all the way down to Jæren's reef.

A piece of the German battleship Tirpitz, 15 centimetres thick, lies beside us.

May 29

We departed from Bergvågen at 2:.45 p.m. and started heading towards Brønnøysund. Logging 7,5 knots and all is well onboard. I am currently in the wheelhouse, leaning out the window. The sun is shining on my face, and I am really enjoying it. We are heading home, at last. Home... some 900 nautical miles away, along one of the most rugged coastlines in the world, but also one of the most beautiful and breath-taking.

The engine was running just fine, but at 3:00 p.m. it suddenly and abruptly shut off! We are a mere six nautical miles away from the town Brønnøysund. The swell is quite heavy with moderate wind.

Slowly, we drifted down Velfjord and would soon be crossing the ferry line between Andalsvågen and Sømna. I rushed down to the engine room and discovered that the forward crank shaft bearing was busted. The axel holding the flywheel was hot as hell and the smell of burnt oil filled the small engine room. The engine was dead stuck, there was no chance we would get it started again.

While I was trying to figure out what to do next, I noticed that the fuel tank was leaking. Small jets of diesel were coming out of the rust holes in the port tank.

I went back up on deck and found the crew was busy trying to hoist the mizzen sail to keep the ship steady and upwind. She was heaving heavily now, facing the waves with her broadside. Seconds later, the mizzen mast falls overboard. I knew it was in poor shape but forgot to share that knowledge with the rest of the crew.

4:15 p.m.

Fired two emergency flares to get the attention of the ferry at Horn. They saw us immediately and came to our rescue, towing us into the ferry pier.

Situation under control.

May 30

At 2:00 a.m., we were awakened by a thumping sound on deck. The chief engineer Asle from the ferry *Kjella* came onboard carrying a huge toolbox. An hour later, after having lifted the heavy flywheel and removing the forward crank shaft bearing, we could safely say that the bearing was badly worn and had to be re-casted.

The crew of *Terje* inhibited a feeling of hopelessness... This was not a good start to our long journey home. Chief engineer Asle read the expressions on our faces and tried to encourage us by saying:

"You can easily get this fixed in Brønnøysund, you can bring it there tomorrow!"

After successfully easing our gloomy minds, he helped us make a dent in some of *Terje's* whisky supply.

Warped *Terje* further down the pier so that we would not be in the way of the morning ferry. Today's distance: 28 nautical miles.

At 9:00 a.m., we hitchhiked to Brønnøysund and had the bearing casted and "chafed". Old bearings are made of bronze halves, the lower half casted with "white metal" and chafed for the shaft to rest upon. The bearing is then lubricated through an oil pipe, feeding oil from a lubricating box to different parts of the engine. If the white metal gets damaged, it must be re-casted and re-chafed.

I was informed that one chafing probably would not be enough.

3:00 p.m., back on the ship testing the bearing but, alas, it needed a do-over… We need to get to the wharf in Brønnøysund.

Filled up the water tank.

May 31

Found out about a suitable tow boat, *M/S Morgen Gry*. Woke up at dawn, being boarded by a big black ship ready to tow us all the way to the wharf in Brønnøysund. At eight knots, with the towing line crackling in a sinister way, we passed North Sømna, Tilrem, and made our way into the bay of Brønnøysund.

I climbed onboard *Morgen Gry* to pay for the towing. The ship was old but in perfect condition, with everything freshly painted. I could not help contemplating all the work that lie ahead of us.

The skipper Arne smiled and his whole face, full of weathered wrinkles from a whole life at sea, lit up as he said:

"No way, not a word of payment! It was my pleasure to be able to help you Swedes!"

"But…"

"You're gonna need your money to get home safely, and that's that. God's speed and good luck to you!"

Seven times the bearing had to be adjusted before it was okay. Got to shower in the local hotel with unspeakable pleasure.

All is well onboard.

June 1

Did a final test run of the engine, and everything seemed to be in order. Left the wharf after trying to pay John, the owner. He would not hear of it!

Set course across the bay of Toftahusen. Just half a mile out, the engine died again.

John had kept an eye on us in his binoculars and came out to tow us back in. The fuel pump and fuel injector were cleaned.

6:00 p.m.

Crew member Per signed off. He had had enough. This last engine failure convinced him that we would never return home alive.

Just the three of us onboard now: Ie, Jan, and I.

Third time lucky – started up and went across the bay for the night. Tomorrow we will install a "new" fuel tank made out of an old gasoline barrel. We moored alongside the trawler *Toftvaer*. The skipper onboard eyed us with some scepticism at first but ended up ordering us to the shower and treating us to a luxurious dinner! The cook onboard *Toftvaer* filled the table with butter-cooked cod and cod liver, home cooked meatballs, salmon, potatoes, and the traditional Norwegian Kneipp bread. The beverage we were served was, of course, tasty Norwegian beer.

The skipper said he wanted to make sure we got back home in one piece, and assured us that he would inform his fishing colleagues along the coast that the Swedes were on their way...

June 2

Incredible breakfast onboard the trawler!

The new tank is in place. Repaired the broken mizzen mast temporarily. Did not get under way until 5:00 p.m. North-westerly winds and heavy seas. Engine running fine and making good headway, logging at 6.9 knots on average. Tired but hopeful.

All is well onboard.

June 3

Left Gerdingen at 10:00 a.m.

Had a visitor in the morning who wanted to know about us and drink our coffee. He contended that *Terje* was worth at least 50,000 crowns…

Leaving Rørvik behind, we entered the open sea. But the seas were heavy, and I became so seasick that I stopped paying attention to the navigation which, after a while, rendered us uncertain of our whereabouts. I could not recognise the landmarks anymore.

The crew insisted that I take a seasick pill. However, since I did not want to leave the wheelhouse as that would make me more nauseous, I had to insert the remedy in my behind. This method is very effective, but awkward. Especially in the narrow and crowded space of the *Terje* wheelhouse, equipped with a long clutch handle, a reversing wheel and, in the back, the radio shelf and chimney from the engine room were lined with a thin layer of insolation and chicken wire. With the engine running, the chicken wire got red hot and kept the wheelhouse warm in cold weather.

Steering a ship in heavy seas while, in a dignified way, inserting a suppository, easily turns into a hilarious balancing act; an act that the woman onboard was willing to ignore by demanding to take the helm while I was doing my thing…

"Please let me take the helm," she pleaded.

"No, I'll handle this!" Not holding the wheel or fixating my gaze on the horizon would probably make me throw up and, like most men, I find the mere thought of throwing up to be intolerable and disgusting. Although I knew it would also be relieving. "And not another word from you!"

Jan, who had overheard what was going on, disappeared down into the engine room with a spasmodic grin on his face.

The task was initiated by using one hand to pull down my pants while keeping the other on the steering wheel. In a half-kneeling position, with one foot in the air, the suppository was successfully put into place. A mere moment later, the ship made a huge roll, and I lost my balance and fell backwards in slow-motion. My vulnerable, naked, protruding body part landed on the chimney and its red-hot chicken wire with a sizzling sound.

The shock triggered an uncontrollable muscle reaction, causing the suppository to shoot out with great force onto the depth finder shelf, which chipped it somewhat, whereafter it finally disappeared into the engine room through a small hole in the floor.

Ie had, without my knowledge, watched the whole thing through the rear wheelhouse window and subsequently hurried down to the crews' quarters while covering her eyes.

I pulled up my pants and swore to never try this again. The pain was immense, and I knew I would have to expose my rear end for treatment as soon as we reached calmer waters. Burns are serious business.

An hour later, we encountered the trawler *Wårsol* who could update us on our position. As it turned out, we had gone much further south than expected. The currents are difficult to predict around here.

Arrived at Hongsand by 7:30 p.m.

My behind was in bad shape and had a reddish grid-pattern which was treated by my crew while they snidely discussed the hazards of suppositories. Alcohol, ointment, and sterile compresses ensured a quick recovery.

Other than that, all is well onboard.

We have decided to only travel during the daytime. Our lanterns are completely useless.

My worry of developing scars on my rear end were unfounded.

June 6

Left Hongsand a little late, at 2:30 p.m. Increasing wind and high seas. The bilge pump broke down, but we fixed it. There is a pump that is powered by the engine, but we still need two pumps working, even though she is not leaking very much.

Trying to fill up our supplies in the small villages along this beautiful coast, but the assortments are very meagre. There is a variety of canned food, including fishcakes and meatballs, but almost no vegetables, not even potatoes.

Moored at Uthaug by 8:30 p.m. There were puffin nests on small shelves on every boathouse. Fantastic birds with colourful beaks!

I have inspected the bows of *Terje* and can establish the fact that she will need a lot of woodwork. Parts of the planking have been washed away by the heavy seas. But one and a half metres from the waterline and below, the planking is fine and without rot.

June 5

The crew of *Terje* are not early risers. Left Uthaug at 1:30 p.m. after refuelling. Beautiful weather! This coast is probably the most scenic in the world. A range of snow-covered mountains follows the coastline continuously. Halfway down, they transform into green forests and pastures, finally ending by the shoreline where the sea rules. Small houses cling to the hillsides, and every farm has its own boathouse down by the fjord. People still live and work here, farming the land, but for how long?

The regulator persists on changing its position while we are under way. The stop screw is worn out, but we fixed it with a piece of wire. While we were passing the Trondheim Fjord, we spotted a Northland Skiff carrying a huge square sail. A sight straight out of the Snorre saga!

Norwegian "Nordlandsjakt"
(Photo unknown)

We are washing our clothes by putting them in a net that is pulled behind the boat, which works well. Currently passing the green, inviting islands of Hitra and Frøya. I hope we can return here some day! We also pass by Terningen lighthouse, situated way out west on a tiny islet which is overpowered by it and the lighthouse keeper's residence. It looks like a stranded ark.

Moored in Kristiansund at 12:30 a.m.

June 6

Strolled around in the harbor all morning and got under way by noon. Pouring rain, everything is damp. Fascinating how water finds its way along beams and planking, just to end up in sleeping bags and on dry clothes.

Almost no wind but a heavy swell. Arrived at Bud by 6:00 p.m.

We finally got the stove working. It resembles a cast iron box on four "legs" and is heated by a genius diesel-dripping system. A copper pipe runs from a small tank on deck down to a faucet. When opened, drops of diesel lands in a funnel, distributing the fuel to a nozzle beneath the stove. A chimney leads the exhaust outside. You light it by filling the stove with paper and opening the faucet just enough for the drops of diesel to start a fire. After a couple of minutes, the oil burns by itself, which creates a pleasant heat in the forecastle. You can forget about fine adjustments; it is all or nothing. But on a day like today the stove is heaven sent, as it helps our sleeping bags and clothes dry up quickly.

What worries me is that there are spots behind the inner wooden lining that never seem to dry up, proven by the fact that my knife easily pierces them all the way through.

An expensive and, according to the farmer we bought it from, freshly slaughtered rooster should be boiled for three hours. In reality, five would be better, but the broth tastes fine already and makes a decent soup. Having it with the last bit of whiskey helps us believe in a safe and happy homecoming.

The engine exhaust pipe has tarred a lot, I must try using a leaner mixture of air and diesel.

June 7

Got under way early! At 9:00 a.m.!

Course set for Stadtlandet, a dreaded passage around an unsheltered peninsula. In fact, it is the only route along this coast where you cannot hide from the Atlantic. Passing Ålesund and Fosnavåg in the afternoon. Hazy weather but calm seas. It is getting colder. By the outskirts of Sandsøy, we decided to try to make it to Årvik before dark, a small village located at the utmost point of the peninsula Stadtlandet. No wind and the forecast promised great weather for tomorrow.

Moored at Årvik by 6:00 p.m. after hesitatingly entering the narrow fjord, a rocky, winding stretch filled with shallows. I must apologise for my negative attitude towards the Norwegian way of marking the sea lanes. In fact, the iron rods are excellent and accurate way finders that make it possible to navigate without charts. They are fitted with arrows that point us in a direction where it is safe to pass, away from the shallows. We moored at the only pier available, well sheltered from the Atlantic swells.

Unfortunately, we are docked right beside the fish factory where they refine fish into fishcakes and fish balls. The waste from the factory is piled onto the pier, awaiting processing into animal feed, and the smell is overwhelming. Decaying intestines emit appalling fumes. A friendly gentleman welcomes us and hands over a few samples of canned goods.

Årvik is a beautiful place, situated between green steep hillsides that are well sheltered from the Atlantic weather. At sunset, we packed a few beers and dried mutton sausages and climbed the ridge, just to get away from the smell. The Norwegian Sea is indescribably beautiful as it rests. The setting sun radiates hues of orange and purple, almost as if it is embracing the universe.

We forget about the beer and sausages as we observe and are blown away by this wonder of nature.

Did not get much sleep this night.

June 8

Woke up to a crystal-clear morning. The warming sun dried the dewy deck and awakened the microbes in the pile of fish entrails. We cast off and left in a haste. The sea is dead calm and the remaining passage around the fearsome Stadtlandet goes swimmingly.

Arrived at Måløysund and bought some fresh buns, cheese, and tomatoes! What a treat. It is becoming easier and easier to find a variety of fresh ingredients the further south we travel.

We carefully passed the infamous "Overhengsklippen" south of Måløysund. It is an enormous piece of a mountain that apparently could come loose at any moment, which would create a disastrous tsunami, capable of flooding the entirety of Måløysund. A huge sign tells us not to sound any horn or fire our ships cannon…

A new daily record of 80 nautical miles today. Moored by an old wooden pier in Austervallshella, a tiny island with its own post office.

June 9

Apparently, we have gotten a taste for early mornings – today we got under way at 7:00 a.m.! The wind is increasing from southwest and, with no sheltering islands windward, we make a stop in Mosterhamn around 11:00 a.m.

It is 2:00 p.m. and the wind has subsided a bit, we are aiming towards reaching Kopervik or even Stavanger by nightfall.

I keep trying to think of a way to cover the holes in the bow. Heavy seas have done a number on the planking, especially on starboard bow. Perhaps plywood would do the job…

Stopped in Haugesund to find charts for the rest of our voyage. As we are running out of money, there is no way we can afford new ones, they are far too expensive. The old ones from the 40s with swastika stamps on them have served us well, but they only go as far as Stavanger.

The crew remained onboard while I visited the fishing trawler by the quay and asked for old charts. I had no luck until I reached the last trawler, *Selvaer of Mosterhamn*, where the skipper had an unconventional solution for my problem. The captain onboard, Ingar Amundsen, informed me that the rest of the Norwegian south coast, all the way to Sweden, is ridiculously easy to navigate…

"You really don't need any charts!"

I objected politely and informed him that I never travelled that way (which was a white lie). He smiled wistfully, as if he considered today's youth a lost generation with a complete lack of intuition.

"Well, well, young lad," he mumbled while lighting a short, stubby pipe and continued:

"I'll just have to draw you a chart then." He sighed and went over to the depth finder to tear off a piece of paper. In less than two minutes, he drew the southern Norwegian coastline, including every lighthouse, all the way to the Swedish coast. All by heart. And his verbal instructions were:

"Now, look here," he paused and exhaled a cloud of smoke resembling a mixture of burning tar and old bilge water, "here you have Jæren's reef and then Egersund, where you can sneak in if the weather gets bad... Further on you can clearly see the church of Kirkehavn, then Vestbygd and Lindesnes. Keep clear of the small island by Ryvingen and then you have arrived at Kristiansand!"

I frantically tried to keep up while taking notes, well aware that our lives depended on getting this right.

His finger left a sooty line on the slip of paper and, every now and then, he added a squiggle with the pencil as he went on:

"The lighthouse on Songvår ... well, even a blind man could see it..." He made a humming sound.

"Now then, if you head north-east all the way past Lillesand and the lighthouse on Homborsund, you can stop by Arendal and buy some beer!" He laughed heartily and emptied his pipe in a piece of iron shrapnel from the war.

"As long as that old Rap hot bulb of yours keeps on running and you head north-east, you'll reach the Swedish coast in no time."

He turned serious, leaned forward, and with a voice that did not allow for any objections, he added:

"You will just have to trust me, young man, I am not kidding around ... I have travelled this coast for 30 years and I know what I am talking about... This is the easiest coastline to navigate in the world, as long as you keep some distance from the shoreline!"

"And, by the way, if there happens to be a rock or shallow in your way, we Norwegians have put an iron rod on top of it with an arrow pointing towards the safe way of passage..." he shook his head and smiled, "and that makes a lot more sense that the Swedish way of using wooden sticks in different colours that are drifting around all over the place... So, if you feel the urge to take a leak on a tuft of grass, just follow the arrows and you'll make port in no time!" He laughed until he coughed, pounded my back, and handed me a sixpack of Ringnes beer as a farewell gift.

As I made my way back to the boat, I decided that I would trust the old fisherman. His genuine experience and knowledge will take us home.

Back at *Terje,* I found my crew standing on the quay and observing the boat with resigned expressions on their faces, their eyes filled with despair.

"What happened?" My voice echoed along the empty pier. They gave no answer, but instead nodded their heads towards the ship. A few seconds later, I noticed the absence of noise from engine. Since we were only staying in Hugesund briefly, I let it run, idling, perhaps at a slightly low rpm. Hot bulb engines could probably run for years on end without a problem, as long as the diesel and lubricating oil keeps on coming. But, if you set it on an rpm that is too low, it will slowly loose some of its compression heat and finally stop. This is what had happened.

The crew, whose knowledge of this engine was limited to how one lubricates it or checks the cooling water, were fully convinced that everything had now come to an end. The old engine had passed away, met its maker, silently gone to rest in the heaven of hot bulbs.

I simply could not resist being their miracle man, nor the "unchallenged, obvious leading figure" of this expedition, so I kept a straight, serious face and snuck into the engine room.

First, I opened the decompression faucet. Then, I turned the flywheel so that the piston was on top in the cylinder, turned on the heating cord, pumped for fuel four times, and turned the lubricator crank handle a few turns. Finally, with a swift push on the compressed air tank, the fly wheel began turning and, after an adjustment on the fuel regulator, the engine levelled out at an even pace.

"Cast off!"

We continued south in the fading light and passed Kopervik, the port where I almost got involved in a mutiny a couple of years earlier. Further on, across the Bokna Fjord and behind Sørbø, we found shelter and anchored for the night.

Additional pieces of the planking have been washed away, and we cannot help wondering if we will get our ship home in one piece.

All is well onboard.

June 11

Left Sørbø at 11:30 a.m.

Hell of a job hoisting the anchor! It weighs about 40 kilos and, combined with 40 metres of a three-quarter inch anchor chain, it takes at least two people to pull it back onboard. But it kept us in place the whole night. The weather is fine, but the seas are heavy. Jan regularly inspects the bows to see how much of them is left...

In sheer amazement, I observe as all of the lighthouses and landmarks keep turning up exactly where captain Ingar placed them on his homemade chart. As the sun sets, we decide on making port at Egersund, following the arrows and markers past reefs and shallows.

By the harbor, a huge deep-sea trawler was unloading its cargo of fresh mackerel. Longing for freshly caught fish and equipped with a plastic bag, we boarded *F/V Shetland*. If we succeed, this will be the first time we have fish for dinner ... in the fishing nation of Norway...

The first mate looked at us as if we were just released from an asylum.

"No, no, I can't sell you any fish ... it's completely against all regulations! We are not allowed to sell fish directly to our consumers!"

We looked at one another and then at the five-ton pile of shimmering mackerel on the pier.

"But…" I resisted the impulse of suggesting where he could put his regulations, and pleaded:

"We just wanted to buy six small mackerels…" The first mate closed his eyes and, with divine patience, ended the conversation by stating:

"You will just have to respect the laws of this country!" And then he disappeared into the bridge.

Deeply disappointed, we cursed the separation of our two nations in 1906. The thought of fresh, fried mackerel and potatoes were going to haunt us for the rest of the day. After returning to *Terje* and praying for *F/V Shetland's* engine to break down windward of Shetland, we suddenly heard a sharp whistle. A short, bearded man with four golden stripes on his uniform appeared on the bridge of the trawler and, reluctantly, we turned back. A plastic bag landed by our feet … filled with fresh shrimp!

"Take all the mackerel you want!" And with that, he was gone.

Afterwards, we spent the evening feasting on seafood. Crispy, fried mackerel with summer potatoes and heaps of melted butter, light Norwegian beer, and heavenly lukewarm shrimp.

June 12

Woke up refreshed and got under way at 8:30 a.m. but encountered very heavy seas. Went leeward of Lædre and spent the day waiting for the seas to calm down. The forecast promised better conditions by 2:00 a.m. but, then again, we had no lanterns.

Feeling frustrated since we are so close to home. There is an abundance of blue shell mussels here, so we had some for dinner. Spent part of the afternoon nailing masonite onto the bow, covering at least the largest holes.

All is well onboard.

June 13

Got under way at 03:15 a.m. Who needs lanterns! The night is light as day. The westerly wind is increasing.

Passed the lighthouses on Lista and Ryvingen. Making nine knots! *Terje* moves well and I know she is going to be a fantastic ship in due time. With a sound hull and sturdy rigg we will travel far with her. I want to have her rigged as a ketch with gaff sails. Above all, I want to return to this coast with her, if not for any other reason than to show her to the Jörgensen brothers. It is going to be a lot of work, but I am sure we will get it done!

By Kristiansand, the south-west swell settled, and the weather became really lovely.

The "chart" is still perfectly accurate and, after having turned north-east at Brekkestø and Homborsund, we moor by Arendal at 6:30 p.m., just in front of the three-mast schooner *The Swan*. Beauty and the beast.

Terje looks like a shabby bilge-rat beside *The Swan*, but that is going to change! An old man from Tjötta came down to see us. He remembered *Terje* from Svinnes!

We have been at sea for 18 days now and travelled 750 nautical miles. All is well onboard, but we are eager to return home, have a decent meal and go for a sauna.

Hopefully the last stretch tomorrow.

June 14

Left Arendal at 7:15 a.m., plotting a course for Risør. The weather is fine and the wind moderate. Seems like we are in a steady, high-pressure area, but the radio broke down, so I could not listen to the weather forecast. After a brief discussion, we finally decided on taking a chance and setting an eastern, 80-degree course straight for Väderöarna in the Swedish archipelago. Clear skies and the wind is just slightly increasing.

Two hours later, the wind picked quickly from south by south-west. Adjusted the course south to make up for the drift.

Wind is increasing even more, and I curse myself for the lack of radio and my own stupidity. The seas are growing rapidly, and I pray for the bows to withstand the beating.

4:30 p.m., semi storm, 24 m/s. Hoisting a small foresail to relieve the starboard bow. Jan reports a heavy leak on the port side just beside the propeller axel, and another one nearby the steering quadrant in the stern. Using both pumps.

Huge seas now, but she is only taking in a small amount of water over the bows. The mizzen mast is on its way overboard again, but we manage to support it with a windward halyard. The engine is running smoothly and we are scouting the hazy horizon, trying to spot the lighthouse on Väderöarna. Suddenly, we discover another landmark – the twin lighthouses on the Koster Islands, far north of our calculated position!

I have underestimated the current and we are now approaching Strömstad, a town not far from the Norwegian border. I have no chart onboard for this part of the coast, but I know most of it anyway. Besides, we have the sun in our back and clear skies, displaying the shoals and shallows as we approach the coastline. Still, just outside Långagärde we almost ran aground on a rock I forgot about... We have shelter from the storm now but decided on continuing past the exposed bay of Kockholmen, just to reach permanent shelter inside the islands.

After nightfall, we reached Havstensund and realised it would be suicide to clear the last distance and round the peninsula Tjurpannan. The storm is raging, making this passage lethal for anything but a pilot cutter.

Disappointed, we moor in Havstensund for the night. So close to home, only a couple of hours left to sail...

Called home and asked them to ready the sauna!

June 15

Still 15-20 m/s, but now coming from north-west. We cast off at 10:00 a.m. and, two and a half hours later, we set anchor in the bay of Lönnholmen. My island, Musön, welcomes us with sunshine and calm seas. 19 days and almost 900 nautical miles later, we are home!

The happy owner
(Photo: the author)

Replacing bad timber
(Photo: the author)

Bow almost done.
(Photo: the author)

Packed in for the winter.
(Photo the author):

Epilogue

For four years she remained a dream, an illusion of endless voyages across the great blue. A lot of work had to be done, including new rib-frames and planking (replacing the ones the Norwegian Sea washed away). Meanwhile, I started a family and moved from the island to a fjord bordering to Norway.

Thereafter, the dream became over-clouded by children and mortgages. During her final winter, she was moored along the old pier by the fjord. That winter was one of the coldest anyone could remember, and I struggled quite a bit to keep her from being crushed by the ice and staying afloat. I waded into the icy water, submerged to my waist, and sealed the leaks, pumped the bilge, and used a chain saw to keep the ice away from the hull.

She was sold for 3500 crowns in June the following year, of which I only received the upfront payment of 1500, and never saw a shadow of the rest.

The new, happy owners enthusiastically engaged themselves in finishing the job I had started. Encouraged by lots of wine and sea shanties, they tore away almost everything I had replaced, but never seemed to correctly replace any of it.

One autumn day, she had disappeared from the boat yard. Gone, vanished from the face of the earth, and nobody could tell me what had happened.

Years later, when I was scouting the coastline for better fishing grounds, I entered a narrow bay just south of the city Strömstad. I rounded a small, rocky point and there, well hidden by hanging bushes, I spotted something sticking up from out of the water. On closer inspection, I could identify what it was; the characteristics of her bow and stern could not be mistaken, it was *Terje*. Slowly, I steered my skiff closer and felt a wave of melancholia come over me. In the clear water, I could clearly discern the rest of her hull as well as the familiar engine room hatch and cargo hold.

In the setting sun, I caught a faint glimpse of the old "Rap" hot bulb engine.

Towing my ship to its new owner
(Photo: unknown)

AFTERWORD

Dear reader,

You have now taken part of some of my adventures at sea onboard ships and boats. Having worked as a professional sailmaker for more than fifty years, there is of course more to depict, more to share, more to remember about all the crazy challenges that has crossed my life's path. A few chapters from the Swedish edition have been left out due to their very local contents.

In the books *"Catalina, travels over land and in the air"* and *"Sea Haze"*, both waiting for translation, I have written about "What happened then?" and some of the supernatural and historic events that occur wherever there is human interaction.

Nowadays I consider myself healed from the urge to live up to the worst challenges and spend my spare time on horseback and in my small double ender, safely moored on my island on the Swedish West Coast.

Northern Sweden January 2024
/Birger Sjöberg

BIBLIOGRAPHY

Short stories:

1. *Tales from the sea* (Prisma/Norstedt Publishing 2001)
   True stories from the seven seas. Adventures for real, voyages and encounters in times before the GPS.

2. *Sea mist* (Norstedt Publishing 2005)
   Short stories from the sea and the Swedish west coast.

3. *Catalina* Short stories (Balkong Publishers 2008)
   Traveling over land and in the air. What happened in America and the love affaire with Golda Meirs cousin.

4. *I embrace your soul* (Norstedts Publishing 2008)
   The story about the mistress of the Swedish poet Evert Taube.

5. *When Goldie Hawn came in from the sea.* (Norstedt Publishing 2009)
   Short stories, true hazardous events, and what to learn from them. How Goldie Hawn came to visit a fisherman a stormy day on the Swedish west coast.

6. *Rigg school* (Norstedt Publishing 2011 Non fiction)
   How to take care of your rigg.

7. *Sailcare* (Norstedts 2011 Non fiction)
   How to take care of your sails.

8. *The adventures of Aunt Anna* (K & R Publishing 2014 fiction children). Based on the life of a lady, her farm, and animals.

9. *The Dragon* (K & R Publishing 2018)
   Short stories, a settlement with the ghosts of the past, guilt and reconciliation.

10. *Boris the Adventures of a Badger*, co-writer Pernilla Magnusson (K & R Publishing 2021)
    The true story about a badger moving in to live with us, and then return to the wild.

Anthologies:

Out at sea (Practical Boatowner Magazine 2004)

Narrators of the sea (Tre Böcker Publishing 2009)

Trample deck (Spencer Unlimited Publishing 2009)

Waves, tales and poetry from the west coast (Recito Publishing *2010)*

Flames, tales and poetry from the west coast (Recito Publishing 2011)

ABOUT THE BOOK

'Tales from the Sea'

Synopsis/review by Journalist Kristine Karlstrom

Should one admit kinship with that rather special race of seafaring humankind, whose hearts beat faster at the sight of a traditional wooden vessel, and a hull whose graceful sheer reflects the beauty of the element which is her home, then one would most likely welcome the chance to escape those long winter evenings which cannot be filled with, linseed-oil, sandpaper and varnish, among the pages of a good book - which means, more or less, something about boats and the sea.

Swedish author Birger Sjöbergs 'Tales from the Sea' is just such a book for fireside reading. Or better still, by the mellow light of a paraffin lamp in the cosy saloon of a pilot-cutter, safely moored, on a dark evening when the Shipping Forecast warns of 'gale force 9 at times'.

A sailmaker by profession with 50 years experience, Stockholm-born Birger Sjöberg lives with his family in northern Sweden sharing his time between writing books, sail making, teaching in a elementary school, and training thirteen horses.

Birger Sjöberg is clearly a mariner who upholds traditional seafaring values and taste and displays a surprisingly 'English' sense of humour. I think he would very probably feel at home in the company of Des Sleightholme, former editor of 'Yachting Monthly'.

In contrast to the hi-tech world of chart plotters and Gore-Tex breathables we meet Birger Sjöberg, dressed in Icelander-pullover, fisherman's oilskins and sporting a pipe. In his own words, an incurable romantic, who ran away to sea at the age of 16, he shares with us in 'Tales from the Sea' his memories of sailing adventures. There we make acquaintance with a colourful gallery of vessels, mostly sailing craft and smaller boats, which have been the (often ungrateful!) objects of his love and affection and carried him on voyages near and far, often with more than his fair, or wished-for, share of drama and excitement. We also meet an equally colourful cast of friends, crewmates, captains, shady characters and memorable chance encounters along the way.

From the charmingly described childhood escapades with a wooden dinghy in the archipelago, Birger Sjöberg makes his way out into the world on the open sea in MS *'Rubens'*. A transatlantic crossing over the threshold of adult sexuality, (he made acquaintance with a young woman who happened to be a cousin of Golda Meir), and into a low-latitude cyclone gusting force 12, and impressing forever upon a blithe and carefree adolescent the awesome majesty and vast potential for violence always latent in the sea, and the absolute need for a sense of humility and respect in the minds of those who sail upon her:

> *"...as we all started to feel it; Rubens had started climbing, as if it were in the grasp of a giant's hand, slowly, in a never-ending motion. Captain De Groote steered straight into the wind and waves, against this south-westerly storm that had originated at Cape Hatteras on the coast of North Carolina. It was building its force and fury now and would not reach its culmination for many hours. The upward motion was overtaken by a heavy roll to port, after which the hull fell forward, picking up an unreal, frightening speed, only to have her ten thousand tons crash into a wall of water at the bottom of the wave. It is meaningless*

to try to attempt describing the sound and feeling of such an impact between steel and water. It must be experienced. Charley was right, this was the end. Finito, bye-bye..."

Thankfully the *'Rubens'* survived her ordeal and Birger Sjöberg lived to tell the tale, though the threat of shipwreck was to follow the young man like a shadow.

A gale just one year later nearly spells the end of the 20m Baltic Trader *'Spirit of Chicago',* and only the timely intervention of the Halmstad pilot-boat saves the vessel from disaster on a lee-shore, after which the author and crew have had enough - the captain proved to be incompetent and somewhat of a psychopath and they count themselves lucky to set foot on 'terra firma' again.

We follow Birger through restoration-projects of hulls whose romantic lines have captured the young man's heart, though most of them have seen better days, some with their future already behind them. As in the 11m former gaff-sloop *'Anna av Risör',* 21-year-old Birger Sjöbergs first 'command' made possible by a timely legacy, but which sadly sinks from under the young skipper's feet in the icy waters of the Kalmar Sound in the Baltic.

Or the 28.5m brigg *'Unicorn',* which survives the elements only to strand upon the reef of betrayal two years later, providing the author with valuable though dearly won insight into human nature.

Adventures in the Caribbean are woven with shorter cameos from home waters, with their own special potential for drama, not least in the winter months and severe cold. Or a chance telephone call summoning Birger to the aid of friends aboard the sixty-year-old *'Tor Helge',* a former 22m Norwegian postal-steamer, bound for the Med. However, after a fire in the engine-room, encounters with German gun-smugglers on board a Colin Archer in Brunsbüttel and with the Dutch Customs and Excise and having seen the inside of a Dutch jail (two bottles of the sealed cargo of spirits being unaccounted for upon arrival in Terneuzen), Birger Sjöberg wisely bids his comrades 'farewell' in Oostende in a tale worthy of the late Tristan Jones.

The author also fulfils an ambition of sailing across the 'pond' from the Canary Islands to the West Indies, which affords him ample opportunity under night-watches to reflect over the vastness of the ocean and the absolute loneliness of a small boat on the open sea:

> *"...Reflecting on the reason for making a voyage like this sometimes overwhelmed us. The loneliness and, above all, the feeling of insignificance brought on by travelling in a fragile man-made shell across a vast ocean, made us aware of our vulnerability. On the ocean's terms, we sailed over depths that could engulf us without a trace. The outcome was dependent our own knowledge and technology, and no mercy could be expected if we made misjudgements or showed a lack of humility..."*

Experience gained on these many and varied voyages and in charter-sailing in the Caribbean lay the foundation for Birger Sjöbergs later career as a professional sailmaker, with his own firm 'Sailmasters', where he serves a clientele from both sides of the Norwegian Swedish border, not only traditionalists, he admits, but also those demanding the latest in sail-technology.

One cannot help a feeling of regret on Birger Sjöberg's behalf, that a significant number of the worthy craft to which he has devoted so many of his younger years have been claimed by the sea. Even the pilot-cutter *'Stout'*, a happy ship which seems to have given the Sjöberg-family much pleasure, was near to disaster, sailing home as she did on Friday the 13th. Birger Sjöberg seems to have something in common with the Canadian author, Farley Mowatt, whose much-loved Newfoundland schooner sank at least three times, if I remember well.

'Tales from the Sea' is not just a collection of yarns about boats but woven into the theme of the sea is the story of the young man's life in the formative years from late adolescence into early manhood. 'Tales from the Sea' therefore offers a wider perspective of interest than the title would suggest. Together with the author's rich descriptive language, vividly capturing the atmosphere and feeling of places, people, and situations, interspersed here and there with his own poetic verse, sense of humour and reflections on life in general, 'Tales from the Sea' should appeal to more than just those who enjoy 'messing about in boats'.

www.ingramcontent.com/pod-product-compliance
Lightning Source LLC
Chambersburg PA
CBHW021627120626
46545CB00002B/431